Praise for *How to Lead by THE BOOK*

"I just read *How to Lead by THE BOOK* and I can clearly understand why my father, Zig Ziglar, endorsed Dave Anderson years ago. Dave's direct, no-nonsense approach to applying Biblical principles to leadership skills is inspiring, encouraging, and literally includes Biblical proportions of leadership wisdom to guide even the most inexperienced leader.

This book should be the foundation, the starting place, for anyone who wants to lead with wisdom far beyond their personal experience.

I couldn't stop highlighting! The leadership wisdom in this book graced every page and gave me new insight about what it truly means to lead.

The whole time I was reading I kept thinking about my father and how much he would love the principles and the stories Dave used to drive home his points. This book has solid, applicable, information that will change your life and the way you lead!"

—Julie Ziglar Norman

How *to* Lead *by* THE BOOK

Proverbs, Parables, and Principles to Tackle Your Toughest Business Challenges

DAVE ANDERSON

WILEY

John Wiley & Sons, Inc.

Published by John Wiley & Sons, Inc., Hoboken, New Jersey.
Published simultaneously in Canada.

Scripture taken from the New King James Version. Copyright © 1982 by Thomas Nelson, Inc. Used by permission. All rights reserved.

Limit of Liability/Disclaimer of Warranty: While the publisher and author have used their best efforts in preparing this book, they make no representations or warranties with respect to the accuracy or completeness of the contents of this book and specifically disclaim any implied warranties of merchantability or fitness for a particular purpose. No warranty may be created or extended by sales representatives or written sales materials. The advice and strategies contained herein may not be suitable for your situation. You should consult with a professional where appropriate. Neither the publisher nor author shall be liable for any loss of profit or any other commercial damages, including but not limited to special, incidental, consequential, or other damages.

For general information on our other products and services or for technical support, please contact our Customer Care Department within the United States at (800) 762-2974, outside the United States at (317) 572-3993 or fax (317) 572-4002.

Wiley also publishes its books in a variety of electronic formats. Some content that appears in print may not be available in electronic books. For more information about Wiley products, visit our website at www.wiley.com.

Library of Congress Cataloging-in-Publication Data:

Anderson, Dave, 1961-
    How to lead by the book : proverbs, parables, and principles to tackle your toughest business challenges / Dave Anderson.
        p. cm.
    ISBN 978-0-470-93628-3 (hardback); ISBN 978-1-118-07517-3 (ebk);
    ISBN 978-1-118-07551-7 (ebk); ISBN 978-1-118-07518-0 (ebk)
        1. Leadership—Religious aspects—Christianity.   2. Personnel management—Religious aspects—Christianity. I. Title.
    BV4597.53.L43A456   2011
    658.4'092—dc22   2010054033

Printed in the United States of America

10 9 8 7 6 5 4 3 2 1

This book is dedicated to Jesus Christ and His persecuted followers in "closed" countries throughout the world, and to exceptional organizations like EQUIP, 222 Ministries, and Voice of the Martyrs, who serve and support them.

Contents

Preface

Every so often, someone comes along and claims that for contemporary times, we need a fresh way to express the Bible's message. Usually that "new" way de-emphasizes Jesus, denies His deity, doubts His resurrection, dangles multiple paths to heaven, disregards biblical inerrancy, disputes the Bible's relevance, and defines grace as license to sin. If you bought this book in hopes of reading any of this nonsense, then you have made a mistake! And, to exact an adequate penalty for pursuing such foolishness, we are keeping your money!

There is no "new" way that I can present the Bible or improve upon its message. The power in its words and truth are unquestionable and unchanging. What I hope to accomplish in *How to Lead by THE BOOK* is to make you more aware of timeless principles that have long existed and to suggest how you can apply them, in practical ways, to improve your life, the lives of others, your business, and our bruised, battered, and beleaguered world. You cannot accomplish this by sitting on the sidelines, reacting to the world around you; rather, you must lead. In this irreverent and irreligious age, leading by biblical principles has never been more necessary or needed.

It is likely that if you are reading this book, you are both a Christian and a leader. Without question, these are complex times for you. Your sense of decency has been besieged by an array of antagonists: indifferent and entitled workers, a generation that dismisses behavioral absolutes, courts and governments that treat religion hostilely and business as an enemy. In the event that some preoccupation has shielded you from observing society's free fall into moral bankruptcy, please take note—as society goes, so go institutions, both for-profit and nonprofit. For starters, consider these eight grim evidences of accelerated cultural decline. Then contemplate the six consequences these corrupt trends will create within your organization.

1. Our national character and reputation are being reduced to the ridiculous. With mendacious media representatives as their wingmen, radical factions in education and government are revising history. They aspire to convince you that our Founding Fathers were godless bumpkins and narcissists, whose original intent was to protect the right to terminate pregnancies, make porn more accessible and prayer less visible, and to reshape marriage to legitimize a behavior God has called abominable. To fully appreciate this particular affront, it helps to understand that the definition of an *abomination* is "abhorrent, disgusting, loathsome, vicious, and vile." Weighing this assault on decency, the words of sixteenth-century theologian

John Calvin describe today's age in terms that are hauntingly precise:

> For it is the summit of all evils, when the sinner is so void of shame, that he is pleased with his own vices, and will not bear them to be reproved, and also cherishes them in others by his consent and approbation. . . . For he who is ashamed is yet healable; but when such impudence is contracted through a sinful habit, that vices, and not virtues, please us, and are approved, there is no more hope of reformation. In Romans, Paul sought to condemn something more grievous and more wicked than the very doing of vices: and that is the casting away of all shame and undertaking the patronage of vices in opposition to the righteousness of God. [Calvin 2005, 19:83]

2. "One nation under God" has become farcical, as activist judges give atheists and agnostics veto power over those who believe in God and support their quest to scrub all evidence of religion from the public square.
3. The escalation of secularism has subordinated God's law to human whims. As a result, moral boundaries have shrunk to the point where the unthinkable has become "normal." Behaviors once publicly decried are now portrayed as acceptable, and those who speak out against them are labeled as bigots.
4. Moral failures among celebrities in sports, business, politics, religion, and even within ordinary families have lost their power to shock us. In fact, it can be argued that one of the greatest tragedies of our time is that we have lost our sense of shame.

5. Hollywood has accelerated its onslaught against God, country, and family values. Television and motion pictures deride Christians, parodying and pillorying them as stiff, fanatical, joyless, peculiar, and unthinking. Conversely, criminals, deviants, atheists, and addicts are represented as cool, witty, intelligent, victimized, free-spirited, and enlightened.

6. To exacerbate the moral confusion, high-profile God mockers and false teachers run rampant among the ranks of best-selling authors, acclaimed comics, entertainment celebrities, church leaders, and business tycoons. For instance:

   • A high-profile media mogul claims that Christianity is a "religion for losers" and labeled his employees as "Jesus freaks" for observing Ash Wednesday.

   • A pastor disgraces Christianity by leading purveyors of hate in nationwide protests brandishing signs declaring: "God hates homosexuals" and "Thank God for dead soldiers."

   • A mega-best-selling book succeeds at duping millions — including Christians — into thinking that the *Law of Attraction* can deliver to them what God cannot or will not.

   • A well-respected talk show host and professed Christian declares there are many more paths to God than Christianity. This generous patron of pie-in-the-sky spirituality sponsors a yearlong "course in miracles" that promotes the opposite of what the Bible calls truth, leading millions astray and into potential destruction with blasphemies like, "There is no sin," "My salvation comes from me," and that "a slain Christ has no meaning."

This pervasiveness of nefarious New Age nonsense has swayed throngs to embrace hellish notions in order to attain success and personal fulfillment. The apostle Paul's 2,000-year-old warning seems designed acutely for our age: *"Now the Spirit expressly says that in latter times some will depart from the faith, giving heed to deceiving spirits and doctrines of demons . . ."* (1 Tim. 4:1).

7. Political correctness has erased all middle ground. You are either pro-choice or a chauvinist, pro-gay rights or homophobic, in favor of affirmative action or a racist, a left coast kook or a right-wing nut. In fact, guard your tongue, because your opinion can as easily be considered hate speech as free speech. Speaking of speech, it is getting uglier. Politicians, pundits, and even ordinary people who disagree about an issue would rather demonize those on the other side than debate them; they'd rather make the conversation personal than talk about principles.

8. The world's acceptance of sinful behaviors has infected religious institutions, some of which celebrate and sanction sinful lifestyles from their leaders under the guise of being loving. Through a shameful distortion of Scripture, fringe factions exploit the love Jesus has for sinners as grounds to assert that He accepts their sins. These divisive strays spin God's Word to appease their carnal appetites, even though church discipline calls for putting out, for the purpose of restoration, those who openly and persistently engage in behavioral turpitude rather than accepting them. Talk about creating confusion, division, and unraveling the moral bounds that have girded civilized culture! When the church itself sanitizes, champions, and validates sin, it surrenders its moral authority as a light unto the world and becomes an enabler to the powers of darkness it was commissioned to oppose.

Like a perfect storm, temporal coalitions in media, education, religion, courts, and government have converged to mock, malign, and mold Scripture to fit and submit to society, rather than using the Bible as a blueprint to shape the culture. By emasculating the Bible to accommodate transgressions, these forces declare that culture has more authority than God's Word, and since culture is determined by human ideas, humans become superior to God.

Not long ago, this contemporary tide to obscure our national memory of its Christian roots would have been unthinkable. However, the forces conspiring to enfeeble our culture seem unwilling to rest until they have exiled God from sight, expunged Him from speech, and supplanted Him with the "gods of this age." This unholy alliance includes, but is not limited to, your school board, legislatures, courts, and federal officials who pine to impose the impious values by which you are to live.

How do the preceding eight cultural trends brutalize your ability to lead effectively? Far more than you might imagine, because trends in organizations have historically followed society's trends. Thus, the ensuing moral collapse of culture impairs your enterprise as follows:

1. Employees are more inclined to emulate the selfish, hedonistic, unethical, and narcissistic behaviors that are ubiquitous and accepted as "normal" in society—and to do so while they are on the job.

2. These behaviors diminish morale, damage your brand, debilitate productivity, and denigrate concern for teammates and customers alike.

3. This in turn increases the likelihood that consumers will develop a greater aversion to dealing with people and buy more online, shopping your prices until your products are commoditized and your margins trivialized.

4. The downward spiral of society's collective character will entice anyone with marginal morals to accelerate the nobbling of their organizations through new and shameless degrees of self-interest, fueled by avarice that would make Bernie Madoff blush.

5. Employees with vulnerable value systems are tougher to manage. They do not believe in absolutes, fail to take responsibility, believe that anything goes, are primarily concerned with themselves, and contend that accountability is unfair. From this, you can expect increased turnover, an escalation of hiring and training costs, diminished team morale, and lower customer retention.

6. The new rules and policies you will need to install to prevent, police, and punish iniquitous behaviors will consume untold time, energy, and financial resources.

These six consequences reflect but a pittance of the hurt you will endure as collateral damage from today's regressive value system cascades and infects all aspects of business and society. As governments, courts, educators, and churches bum-rush Scripture and dumb down decency in surrender to tolerance, a population conditioned to thumb its nose at God will sink further into the emptiness of secularism. With pitiable values steeped in hedonism, a surging sector will worship at the altar of selfishness, self-indulgence, and ease, engaging in anything, and falling for everything, because they stand for nothing.

As you endure the deterioration of individual character and degradation of corporate ethics, there are important questions to consider:

- How can you succeed in building and sustaining a character-driven culture in your organization?

- How do you buck the trend toward hypertolerance and "anything goes" that has the potential to create a culture of chaos in every entity in which you play a role (home, work, community, or church)?
- Is it any wonder that leaders who endeavor to make a positive difference in their business, church, community, government, and family become frustrated, frightened, and fraught with stress when facing such formidable foes?
- Where do you turn for straight answers, without the spin and stench of political correctness?
- Which success principles are still absolute and unimpeachable despite the times, circumstances, and the tug of cultural currents, and where can you find them?

I believe you know the answer to the last question, and that is why you have invested in this book. You want it to reaffirm what you intuitively, if not wholeheartedly, assert to be true: God's Word remains authoritative and relevant, it still brings life, and it is futile to waste time chasing leadership fads, gurus, "secrets," or flavors of the month that offer shortcuts, substitutes, or alternatives to proven practices rooted in biblical truth.

Perhaps you have even experimented with New Age approaches to spirituality, leadership, or personal development in your own organization and are ready to return to real truth. If so, be heartened by the words of C. S. Lewis: "We all want progress. But progress means getting nearer to the place where you want to be. And if you have taken a wrong turn, then to go forward does not get you any nearer. If you are on the wrong road, progress means doing an about-turn and walking back to the right road; and in that case the man who turns back soonest is the most progressive man" (Lewis 2001, 28).

The best book ever created on leadership principles, the Bible, was inspired by God, is inerrant in nature, and offers us nothing less than an incomparable slice of God's own mind! The Bible packs a punch with sufficient power to overcome any prejudiced media, hostile government, cowardly court, atheist's rant, secular assault, or false teacher's philosophy. In an age where we are encouraged to judge and discriminate against nothing and to tolerate everything except intolerance, principled men and women should be steadied by the fact that the Bible promotes the intolerance of numerous behaviors, and it is brutally judgmental and discriminatory wherever unholy ethos are concerned. Try John 3:18 and Acts 4:12, for example. Frankly, your character as a leader is largely defined by what you *do* judge as wrong and discriminate against and by what you *will not* tolerate.

Despite the Bible's potential to reshape your business, life, and society, it cannot help you if you do not know, accept, and apply its truths. However, before you can employ the Bible, you must first understand what it says about how to live and lead according to God's plan. That is where I endeavor to serve as your guide through the chapters of this book. For starters, regardless of your past personal or business behaviors, THE BOOK is rife with promises of grace and redemption: *"Then you will know the truth and the truth will set you free"* (John 8:32); *"For whoever calls upon the name of the Lord will be saved"* (Romans 10:13); and *"... neither do I condemn you, go and sin no more"* (John 8:11).

My purpose in writing *How to Lead by THE BOOK* is to equip you to live and lead a more robust life, all while you exponentially elevate organizational results. The principles I present transcend factors like age, education, religion, gender, or political affiliation. While Christians will more readily recognize the New Testament strategies, readers of all faiths will benefit by applying the timeless truths and tenets within these pages.

What is truly exciting is that by using the Bible as your leadership playbook, you have an incredible wealth of wisdom at your disposal. The Protestant Bible is made up of 66 books, 1,189 chapters, 31,173 verses, and 773,692 words! The strategies I present in *How to Lead by THE BOOK* will touch on only a token of what the Bible imparts, but they will more than suffice to transform your life and business as you apply them. You may be familiar with many of the proverbs, parables, and principles that I have included. Whether you have applied and are benefiting from their power may be something else altogether. To this end, I will nudge, cajole, and persuade you to *act* to close the gulf of unfulfilled potential that lies between knowing what to do and actually doing it.

I encourage you to read, *How to Lead by THE BOOK* cover to cover and then to refer to it often as a desk reference. I address 14 of your toughest business challenges in this book, and I conclude with a short chapter called "Closing Thoughts." I suggest that you search the Bible for additional insights into each of the topics I present. Because of space constraints, I could not possibly list all that the Bible says about each issue. Thus, keep in mind that what I present is the alpha and not the omega.

I introduce each of the 14 challenges in a stand-alone chapter using the following format:

1. A description of the challenge
2. A presentation of "Man's Wisdom and Ways" for handling the issue
3. An outline of "THE BOOK's Wisdom and Ways" for meeting the challenge, including precise biblical references, personal experiences, and real-life examples of the strategy in action
4. Close each challenge with an "Omega" section containing steps and relevant scriptures relating to obedience and follow-through

A common question I encountered during press interviews in the wake of publishing my last book, *How to Run Your Business by THE BOOK* was, "Is the entire Bible relevant and practical, or are some parts not worth worrying about?" Be assured that the entire Bible is useful, practical, and powerful! As proof, I have included strategies, scriptures, and precepts from a vast array of biblical books. Through years of studying and applying biblical wisdom, I have discovered this simple fact: The verse you do not read cannot help you, and the principle you fail to apply cannot change your life.

The downward spiral of society's morality and its accompanying consequences that I enumerated at the outset of this preface are frighteningly real and cannot be combated by lip service. Thus, my prayer is that as you read this book, the biblical principles will cause you to experience the same sensation enjoyed by the disciples on the road to Emmaus as Jesus spoke with them about God's word following His resurrection—and that your mind will be transformed, your leadership reenergized, and your impact multiplied: *"And they said to one another, 'Did not our heart burn within us while He talked with us on the road, and while He opened the Scriptures to us?'"* (Luke 24:32).

A final word: Do not make the error of underestimating the potential power of biblical principles to help you *immediately*! As in John 11:23–24, when Martha affirmed to Jesus that she believed He would raise her dead brother Lazarus "in the resurrection on the last day," and Jesus called Lazarus forth from the grave *at that moment*, so, too, will you discover, as she did, that God's power operates in the *present* and is not reserved for some future time or age.

Acknowledgments

It gives me great pleasure to acknowledge the following family, friends, and colleagues who have helped me with this book:

- To Rhonda, my wife and business partner. You are the love of my life, and if you ever leave me, I am going with you!
- To Russell, for your exceptional work running LearnToLead with Rhonda so that I had the time to write this book.
- To Ryan, for your diligent labors in proofing and formatting this book . . . and for tolerating the many, "Oh, by the way, could you add this to chapter so-and-so" after it was already complete.
- To Dan and Matt at John Wiley & Sons, for your enthusiasm and support for the *By THE BOOK* brand.

- To my beautiful and brilliant daughter Ashley, for your recommendations, which I have happily included. How did you get so smart?
- To Christian giants of faith like Spurgeon, Simeon, Henry, and Gothard, who have added incredible richness to my understanding of the Scriptures.

How *to* Lead
by THE
BOOK

How Do I Hold People Accountable?

MAN'S WISDOM AND WAY

Get in their face with tough talk. Intimidate, threaten, and bully. If they don't like it, they should either step up or opt out!

In the 1,000 leadership presentations I give each decade, I have discovered that this old-school palaver is still the strategy of choice for many misguided leaders. While trying to find the right word to describe this tendency herein, I could not decide whether to use *hopeless*, *futile*, or *stupid*. Thus, I have decided to define this method for accountability as *hopelessly futile stupidity*.

THE BOOK'S WISDOM AND WAY

Keys to holding others accountable include clear feedback on performance and consequences for failing to perform. These topics are covered in future chapters. But before we get ahead of ourselves, it's important to remember the first nonnegotiable for accountability: You can't first hold others accountable until you're resolutely clear about what you expect from them!

While visiting the Mount of Beatitudes in Israel, I was struck by its prominence in height and stature compared to its surroundings. Thus, it is fitting that Jesus chose this spot to teach on the topic of elevated values and expectations. In Matthew 5–7, Jesus outlined the revolutionary values of the Christian faith with His Sermon on the Mount. He presented clear behavioral standards, along with appropriate rewards or penalties, contingent upon one's obedience. Whereas the Old Testament ended in Malachi 4:6 with a curse, Jesus began His ministry teaching on the Mount with a blessing: *"Blessed are the poor in spirit for theirs is the kingdom of heaven."* You are able to bless your employees in a similar manner when you clearly define what you expect from them. You simultaneously strengthen your organization, as doing so provides an essential benchmark for accountability.

Why did Jesus set forth expectations and values so early in His ministry? For the same reason you must do so within your organization: You cannot possibly hold anyone accountable until you define what you expect in the first place! But even more important, it gave Him a chance to model what He expected with His own life. Even when Jesus's mouth was closed, He taught by His life. You must do likewise. After all, you cannot credibly hold others accountable for the behaviors you have defined as nonnegotiable unless you personally live them.

There is no record in Matthew of Jesus offering feedback to anyone, much less holding them accountable, until He had clearly defined what He expected from his followers. Using THE BOOK as a guide, consider the seven thoughts and rules in this chapter to help you create a higher-accountability culture in your organization.

Some leaders believe that establishing clear, high, written expectations is harsh and is a form of micromanagement; therefore, they present their expectations punctuated with an apology. On the contrary, what is truly harsh is *not* letting people know what you expect and allowing them to fail. Thus, if you want to apologize for something, apologize for letting others flounder and drift, but never for being clear about what you expect from them.

1. Ambiguity is the enemy of accountability.

Until you define or redefine expectations for technical and behavioral performance on the job, holding others accountable is unfair and impossible, because the question becomes, "Accountable for what?"

2. Failing to communicate the truth of expectations and accountability to your associates puts "blood on your hands" when you terminate them and they don't see it coming.

If you catch employees by surprise when you fire them, you have failed as a leader. You either failed to set clear expectations, failed to give honest feedback on their performance, or failed to hold them accountable throughout their tenure with your organization. The Bible relates a parallel situation when God instructs Ezekiel to act as a watchman for his contemporaries. In a similar manner, you serve as the watchman for any entity in which you wish to exhibit leadership.

> Son of Man, I have made you a watchman for the house of Israel; therefore hear a word from My mouth, and give them warning from Me: When I say to the wicked, 'You shall surely die,' and you give him no warning, nor speak to warn the wicked from his wicked way, to save his life, that

same wicked man shall die in his inquiry, but his blood I will require at your hand. Yet, if you warn the wicked, and he does not turn from his wickedness, nor from his wicked ways, he shall die in his iniquity; but you have delivered your soul. [Ezek. 3:17–19]

3. **Giving honest feedback, as fast after a behavior as possible, is a key to eliminating gray areas and holding others accountable.**

No one working with you should ever have to guess where they, or you, stand concerning your expectations or their performance. Give fast, honest, specific feedback to reinforce productive actions and confront errant behaviors.

4. **Consequences for failing to perform must be established and imposed.**

In Matthew 25, you read about the Parable of the Talents. A talent was the largest measure of money in the Greek system. The unprofitable servant had his one talent taken from him—the one he refused to use—and given to the top performer, who had increased his five talents to ten! His penalty for not using the opportunity he had been given was to lose it. Even though this "one talent" servant was trusted with less than the others, he was still accountable for what little he was given. As is typical of those failing to deliver results, this underachiever casually attempted to excuse burying his talent, almost as though he were expecting praise for his prudence in preserving rather than increasing it. To exacerbate matters, he made light of his sloth by uttering an excuse and blaming the master who had entrusted him with the talent: *"Sir, I knew you to be a hard man, reaping where you have not sown, and gathering where you have not scattered seed. And I was afraid, and went and hid your talent in the ground"* (Matt. 25:24–25).

Like the master in this story you must "coach with consequences," enriching those who deliver results and punishing the sluggards falling short. Without consequences for failing to reach established performance standards, those standards are reduced to suggestions, and your personal credibility is rendered ridiculous.

In the first book of Corinthians, chapter 5, Paul is writing about sexual immorality and its consequences. It seems as though a church member was sleeping with his father's wife. Note that Paul gives no apology for the consequence. The fellow who was living in sexual sin was to be put out of the church, and suffer for lack of its fellowship, until he had repented and was spiritually restored. Paul rightly reasoned that condoning someone who publicly persisted in such scandalous sin could corrupt the entire body of believers in Corinth. Then, as now, professing Christians are on public display. Those who confess Christ with their lips, but deny Him with their lifestyle, do incalculable damage to Christ's cause. Read these words from the apostle Paul concerning this accountability issue:

> It is actually reported that there is sexual immorality among you, and such sexual immorality as is not even named among the Gentiles—that a man has his father's wife! And you are puffed up, and have not rather mourned, that he who has done this deed might be taken away from among you. For I indeed, as absent in body but present in spirit, have already judged (as though I were present) him who has so done this deed. In the name of our Lord Jesus Christ, when you are gathered together, along with my spirit, with the power of our Lord Jesus Christ, deliver such a

one to Satan for the destruction of the flesh, that
his spirit may be saved in the day of the Lord Jesus.
[1 Cor. 5:1–5]

It is essential that your team members are taught that when
they choose a behavior, they are also choosing the consequences
for that behavior. They should not consider themselves as victims.
Rather, they're reaping what they've sown. In fact, the behavior/
consequence connection works both ways: Choose a productive
behavior and earn a positive consequence. Choose an unproductive behavior, and you will reap the penalty you have sown for
yourself. What could be fairer?

**5. Expectations are easily forgotten. Thus, the leader must
live them and repeat them often.**

Just about the time you tire of repeating an expectation is when
others are beginning to *get* it. Never fear that you will overcom-
municate any aspect of clarity to your people. It will not happen.
Following are three examples.

- **The Ten Commandments (×2)**

The Ten Commandments were first given in Exodus 20. They
were reviewed again in Deuteronomy 5, albeit to a new generation. Moses did not rely on his followers' memories or on what
may have been passed down to them from their ancestors. He
erred on the side of "repetition brings retention."

- **Finders Keepers (×2)**

In John 14:21, Jesus said: *"He who has My commandments and keeps
them, it is he who loves Me. And he who loves Me will be loved by My Father,
and I will love him and manifest Myself to him."* One chapter later,

in John 15:10, Jesus declared to the same group of disciples: *"If you keep My commandments you will abide in My love, just as I have kept My Father's commandments and abide in His love."*

The Bible is filled with repetition, not because the authors forgot they stated these words, but because they are important! Especially in today's age of "it is not my fault," you must work doubly hard to eliminate the excuses of, "I did not know that was what you wanted," "I can't read your mind," and the like.

- **Sexual Immorality (×3)**

In just a single chapter of 1 Corinthians, Paul warns of sexual immorality three times! He made it impossible for anyone to play dumb or say, "I wonder what the church has to say about sexual immorality?"

- *"Do you not know that the unrighteous will not inherit the kingdom of God? Do not be deceived. Neither fornicators, nor idolaters, nor adulterers, nor homosexuals, nor sodomites, nor thieves, nor covetous, nor drunkards, nor revilers, nor extortioners will inherit the kingdom of God"* (1 Cor. 6:9–10).
- *"Now the body is not for sexual immorality, but for the Lord, and the Lord for the body"* (1 Cor. 6:13).
- *"Flee sexual immorality. Every sin that a man does is outside the body, but he who commits sexual immorality, sins against his own body"* (1 Cor. 6:18).

Even if they get it, repeat it to reinforce it.

It is estimated that Paul spent only a few weeks or months in the city of Thessalonica (now called Salonica) in modern-day Greece, before being run out of town by the Jewish leaders who opposed his teachings. Thus, some of his earliest letters were written to the Thessalonian churches to reinforce his teachings, and encourage the new Christians there. In fact, after his letter to the Galatians, 1 and 2 Thessalonians were the earliest letters written by Paul. (Contrary to what many assume, the letters of Paul are not listed in chronological order in the New Testament.) It was obvious that Paul believed the Thessalonians knew about brotherly love and lived accordingly; however, he felt compelled to repeat the expectation anyhow, in order to support and advocate more of the same behavior. *"But concerning brotherly love you have no need that I should write to you, for you yourselves are taught by God to love one another; and indeed you do so towards all the brethren who are in all Macedonia. But we urge you, brethren, that you increase more and more. . . ."* (1 Thess. 4:9–10).

When it comes to your vision, values, mission, and performance expectations, err on the side of overcommunication with your words and by your deeds.

6. Expectations should be visible, in writing, and communicated through various mediums.

Human beings tend to manipulate gray areas to rationalize or excuse their failure to perform. Point 6 goes a long way in helping you to eliminate this possibility.

In Deuteronomy 6, God topped off the Ten Commandments Moses had just reviewed in Deuteronomy 5 with the greatest commandment: *"You shall love the Lord your God with all your heart, with all your soul, and with all your strength"* (Deut. 6:5).

He then instructed as follows: *"And these words which I command you today shall be in your heart. You shall teach them diligently to your children, and shall talk of them when you sit in your house, when you walk by the way, when you lie down, and when you rise up. You shall bind them as a sign on your hand, and they shall be as frontlets between your eyes. You shall write them on the doorposts of your house and on your gates"* (Deut. 6:6–9).

You can make expectations visible, credible, and memorable in the following ways:

- Discuss them both publicly and one-on-one.
- Publicly commend those who fulfill an expectation.
- Evaluate employees against them during performance interviews.
- Put them in writing and go over them with each employee. Require each team member to sign off to acknowledge that they understand what is expected and affirm that you and they are on the same page.

7. **Accountability is ineffective when you use it as a tool to try to trick or strong-arm the *wrong* person into doing the *right* thing.**

You can't trick the wrong people into being competent. This is because empowering them with clear expectations and providing them with the training, resources, and opportunities to attain the established objectives will not improve their moral character. In other words, accountability is not a strategy for tricking a corrupt person into behaving rightly!

I cover this topic more thoroughly in Chapter 4, which relates to hiring the right people. For now, it is important to understand that if you do not start with employees who have the right character, then training them, giving them direction, and holding them accountable will not improve them or their performance in any sustainable manner.

Judas was not inferior in knowledge or miracle-working power to the other disciples. He had the same opportunities to grow, perform, and develop spiritually as his 11 counterparts; however, Jesus's clear expectations, training, positive example, and accountability did not penetrate an unyielding and willful heart, determined to rot in its own corruption. On the contrary, Judas developed a greater guilt for neglecting to use what he was given, and he ultimately became the most shameful disciple. Without the right moral foundation, your ethically challenged employees cannot be expected to excel, despite the high degree of accountability you have as the centerpiece of your culture. A morally corrupt employee is far more likely to shape your culture than your culture is to change his or her wrong and inflexible heart.

As you can see, if you are going to hold others accountable by THE BOOK, your first responsibility is to create clarity. This would be an appropriate time to honestly evaluate clarity of expectations within your enterprise. As basic as this seems, it is essential to creating a high-performance culture rooted in strong accountability. Incidentally, if you're not certain whether your expectations are specific and high enough, they're not!

Consider the following Omega thoughts and Scriptures, chosen because they relate specifically to the topic of this chapter.

OMEGA

"And the Lord said to Moses, 'Whoever has sinned against Me, I will blot him out of My book. Now therefore, go, lead the people to the place of which I have spoken to you. Behold, My Angel shall go before you. Nevertheless, in the day when I visit for punishment, I will visit punishment upon them for their sin'" (Exod. 32:33–34).

1. The only way you will have credibility when holding others accountable for your expectations and values is if you personally live them! Your words and deeds must be in alignment. If your organization has clear performance and behavioral standards, how consistently do you live them? If you "talk right and walk left," you'll leave your people behind.

2. What is your first step to create a higher-accountability culture?

"I am the vine, you are the branches. He who abides in Me, and Me in him, bears much fruit; for without me you can do nothing. If anyone does not abide in Me, he is cast out as a branch and is withered; and they gather them and throw them into the fire, and they are burned" (John 15:5–6).

Is It Right to Hold Leaders More Accountable than Followers?

MAN'S WISDOM AND WAY

Leadership is about privileges. Once you pay your dues and "arrive," you're not subject to the same demands or expectations as followers. There is an unspoken understanding that organizational rules and values are designed to keep the flock in line; they don't apply equally to leaders.

It is within the realm of reason to claim that there is scarcely a person on the planet who has not been in some way impacted by the arrogance and sense of entitlement demonstrated by those who embody the preceding approach to leadership. Whether in business, politics, church, or the average household, selfish and prideful leaders debilitate and destroy companies, countries, denominations, and families.

THE BOOK's Wisdom and Way

Is it right to hold leaders more accountable than followers? The following words of Jesus quickly answer the question, *"Everyone who has been given much, much will be demanded; and from the one who has been entrusted with much, much more will be asked"* (Luke 12:48).

The apostle Paul, when writing about church leaders in his letter to Timothy, ordered: *"Those who are sinning rebuke in the presence of all, that the rest also may fear"* (1 Tim. 5:20).

There is always more riding on the quality of a leader's performance than on the performance of those at lower levels. In fact, when an organization is struggling or underachieving, you should not first try to fix it in the middle or at the bottom of the organizational ladder; rather, you fix it at the top. This is because the old saw is true: *A fish rots at the head—it starts to stink at the top first!*

I was asked at a seminar whether a poorly performing manager should be given more or less time to get results than an underachieving subordinate. I suggested that bad leaders should be given less time and less rope, because when they hang themselves, they take many other people down with them. I have heard business owners declare that in order to rid themselves of poorly performing managers, they need only to give them enough rope and they will hang themselves. This is a flawed philosophy! When you give poor managers enough rope, they will tie you up, plunder your enterprise, and leave you and your organization for dead! In order to lead by THE BOOK, you must resolve to hold leaders to a far higher standard than their followers.

A LEADER'S FAILURE AFFECTS MORE PEOPLE THAN A FOLLOWER'S

You must demonstrate less tolerance for slackers in leadership because there is more at stake for the organization: team morale, momentum, market share, the corporate culture, and more. In fact, nothing diminishes an organization faster than an ineffective leader. A leader's incompetence or weak character has a devastating impact on people, culture, momentum, and morale. In Hosea 13:11, God declared that He had punished Israel by giving its people an inept king. Proverbs 29:2 promises, *"When the righteous are in authority, the people rejoice; but when a wicked man rules, the people groan."*

If you have ever worked for an incompetent or corrupt leader, I do not need to tell you that your work life becomes misery on the installment plan!

CORRUPT LEADERS ARE AGENTS OF SIN

In some cases, leaders demonstrate competence but lack character. These rascals are even worse than the totally incompetent. If, God forbid, a leader lacks both character and competence, the organization doesn't stand a chance! There is a litany of lousy kings listed in the Old Testament in the first and second books of Kings. The ineffective king is normally introduced into a chapter with a disclaimer similar to this: *"And he did evil in the sight of the Lord; he did not depart from the sins of Jeroboam the son of Nebat, who has made Israel sin"* (2 Kings 14:24).

The final five words of this Scripture explain the immense stakes involved when a leader has character flaws: Weak character at the top of an organization can serve as a corporate contagion.

15

WHEN THE LEADER SLEEPS, THE TEAM FOLLOWS

Peter's name is mentioned in the Gospels more than any other name except Jesus. He was the leader of the disciples, and a member of Jesus's inner circle, along with John and James. In Mark 14:32, Jesus and the disciples had just finished the Last Supper, sung a hymn, and gone out to the Mount of Olives. While there, Jesus told them that they would all be made to stumble because of Him that night. Despite Peter's protestations, Jesus predicted that Peter would deny Him three times that very evening. Thus, as they ventured into the Garden of Gethsemane, there was no doubt a lot on their minds.

> Then they came to a place which was named Gethsemane; and He said to His disciples, "Sit here while I pray." And He took Peter, James and John with Him, and He began to be troubled and deeply distressed. Then He said to them, "My soul is exceedingly sorrowful, even to the death. Stay here and watch." He went a little farther, and fell on the ground, and prayed that if it were possible, the hour might pass from Him. And He said, "Abba, Father, all things are possible for You. Take this cup away from Me; nevertheless, not what I will, but what You will." Then He came and found them sleeping, and said to Peter, "Simon, are you sleeping? Could you not watch one hour? Watch and pray, lest you enter into temptation. The spirit indeed is willing, but the flesh is weak." [Mark 14:32–38]

Jesus found all three disciples sleeping. These three, who had so vehemently insisted previously that they were ready to share His sufferings and would never deny Him, were so unconcerned by their Master's sorrow and pain that they slept while He agonized and prayed. Luke's account details that Jesus was so distressed, He sweat drops of blood—while His three key men took a nap!

Yet when Jesus found his inner circle in slumber, He did not address all three by name, only Peter. Why? Peter was the leader. Jesus expected more from him. After all, he boasted the loudest about his fidelity only a few moments prior, in Mark 14:31, when he vehemently spoke the words, *"If I have to die with You, I will not deny You!"*

The lesson here is clear: When the leader sleeps, so does the team. If a leader catches a cold, you can expect the followers to come down with pneumonia. This is precisely why leaders must be held to a higher standard than those they lead—in businesses, churches, governments, and families.

THE BUCK STOPPED WITH ADAM

In the third chapter of Genesis, God had given clear instructions to Adam and Eve not to eat the fruit of a certain tree in the Garden of Eden. After the serpent convinced Eve to violate God's instructions and sample the goods, Eve then invited Adam to do likewise. Matters unraveled from there, as God asked a question we must all answer one day: *"Have you eaten from the tree of which I commanded you not to eat?"* (Gen. 3:11).

Technically, Eve sinned first. However, Adam is the one held accountable throughout the Scriptures for bringing sin into the world, because he was the spiritual leader of the couple and was thus responsible. In fact, at the moment when God asked the question and Adam proceeded to blame Eve, Eve had not even been named yet! She was still referred to as, "the woman." Adam's refusal to take a stand in the face of "the woman's" invitation to sin

17

caused Paul to write in Romans 5:12, *"Therefore, just as through one man sin entered the world and death through sin. . . ."* Paul does not even mention Eve, because Adam, as the leader, was responsible. He knew better, but he did not do better.

While both Adam and Eve suffered consequences for their sin, the buck stopped with Adam. This was despite his wretched attempt to blame his mate. To exacerbate his predicament, he even blamed God Himself. When asked whether he had eaten the forbidden fruit, Adam told God: *"The woman whom You gave to be with me, she gave me of the tree, and I ate. . . . Eve then bequeathed the blame down to the serpent by whining, 'The serpent deceived me, and I ate'"* (Gen. 1:12–3:13).

Neither Adam nor Eve repented, apologized, or accepted responsibility; rather, they pointed, blamed, spun, and hid—a trend that their descendants follow en masse today.

LEADERSHIP IS NOT ABOUT RIGHTS, IT IS ABOUT RESPONSIBILITIES

With power comes responsibility. Leaders are expected to know better and do better than followers. As a result, they are not only held to a higher level of accountability, but likewise expected to endure a greater degree of punishment for not doing what is right. Consider the words of Jesus as reported by Luke: *"And that servant who knew his master's will, and did not prepare himself or do according to his will, shall be beaten with many stripes. But he who did not know, yet committed things deserving of stripes shall be beaten with few. For everyone to whom much is given, from him much will be required; and to whom much has been committed, of him they will ask the more"* (Luke 12:47–48).

Christian leaders must rise to the occasion and remember that they belong to God. They must acknowledge the wisdom, power, mercy, and grace they have been given and the sacrifice made for them. With freedom in Christ comes more responsibility to others—and a far higher standard to strive toward than that aspired to by those living according to the world's standards.

Following are four examples of leaders to whom much was given, and how they were held accountable by God.

THE RICH MAN GOES TO HELL

According to the Bible, the expanding slew of corporate leaders that pilfer their company's treasures, deplete shareholder value, betray their hardworking associates, and compromise their character for cash should be beaten more severely! Unjustly, many of these malefactors are enriched with multimillion-dollar exit prizes as they are booted from their looted employers. If you have ever felt entitled or comfortable as a leadership glutton, believing you have gotten away with your sin, or if you have suffered torment as the victim of these monsters and believed that your oppressor's wealth or status created a chasm that separated him or her from the law or from accountability in general, you may wish to revisit Jesus's teaching story of the rich man and Lazarus in Luke 16:19–31.

The rich man enjoyed all that could gratify an earthly mind and, after a short enjoyment of his worldly pleasures, was doomed to an eternity in hell. He had been financially blessed by God, but failed to respond in humility or belief. Despite his apparent single-minded pursuit of wealth, it is safe to surmise he was never satisfied, because, as Ecclesiastes 5:10 warns, *"He who loves silver will never be satisfied by silver; nor he who loves abundance with increase. This also is vanity."*

Lazarus was the beggar, full of sores, who daily panhandled for crumbs. THE BOOK tells us that after a transient stint of suffering on earth, he was transported by the angels to a state of everlasting bliss. Here is an excerpt that portends how one's earthly comforts can turn into eternal torment and how one's temporary torment one day transcends to continuous comfort. Lazarus may have been an actual person that Jesus used as an example, since none of His other teaching stories or parables mention a specific name.

> So it was that the beggar (Lazarus) died and was carried by the angels to Abraham's bosom. The rich man also died and was buried. And being in torment in Hades, he lifted up his eyes and saw Abraham afar off, and Lazarus in his bosom. Then he cried and said, "Father Abraham, have mercy on me, and send Lazarus that he may dip the tip of his finger in water and cool my tongue; for I am tormented in this flame." But Abraham said, "Son, remember that in your lifetime you received your good things, and likewise Lazarus evil things; but now he is comforted and you are tormented. And besides all this, between us and you there is a great gulf fixed, so that those who want to pass from here to you cannot, nor can those from there pass to us."
> [Luke 16:19–31]

The rich man did not go to hell because he was rich. In fact, the Bible does not tell us precisely why he went to hell. However, knowing the character of both humans and God, we may deduce that possibly his riches became his god, causing him to obtain them, increase them, and protect them in a manner that dishonored God and abused people. As we see repeatedly throughout the Bible, to whom much was given, much was expected, and the consequences for failing to step up and deliver were severe—and should remain so today within your own organization.

THE SCRIBE'S POWER PLAY REBUFFED

While you peruse the following passage from Matthew, read between the lines to discern what the scribe's probable motive was in wanting to become Christ's follower: *"Then a certain scribe came and said to Him, 'Teacher, I will follow You wherever You go.' And Jesus said to him, 'Foxes have holes and birds of the air have nests, but the Son of Man has nowhere to lay His head'"* (Matt. 8:19–20).

The scribe wanted to follow Jesus, but undoubtedly expected superior treatment and regard because of his position. Jesus told him that even He, as the Master, had surrendered His rights and was without a place to call home. Jesus wanted the scribe to understand that as a leader, He had given up His rights in order to serve, and the scribe should expect to do likewise. Matthew does not elaborate about how the scribe responded. My guess is that he decided to stick with scribing, where he could continue to leverage his position for perks.

400 YEARS OF THE SILENT TREATMENT

Has God ever given you the silent treatment? If so, you are not alone. Take a look at what happened to the nation of Israel when God had had enough of their nonsense. Malachi is the final book of the Old Testament, named for a prophet who served during Nehemiah's day. His name means, "Messenger of Yahweh"—and Malachi's message was right in the leader's faces as he attacked their moral and spiritual decay. Malachi used a unique method of speaking and teaching, whereby he would make a charge, raise potential objections, and then refute them. This didactic-dialectic method of speech denounced the leaders—priests and others—who had become the ultimate hypocrites. They had gotten comfortable engaging in egregious behavior: mistreating their wives, robbing God with their offerings, partaking in mixed marriages and rampant divorce, profaning the sanctuary, and promoting false teaching. God's disgust with these so-called leaders had reached its limit. The result? Centuries of divine silence followed the book of Malachi as God refused to speak to His people through a prophet until John the Baptist arrived on the scene 400 years later! Again, an entire people suffered because the leaders, from whom much was expected, lacked both character and competence.

PAUL'S CALL TO STEP UP

I had the pleasure of visiting Ephesus, Turkey, and touring its stunning ruins. I can understand why the apostle Paul saw so much potential in this vital area and invested key years of his ministry there.

After building the church at Ephesus and running a small seminary there to groom future leaders, Paul gave his farewell speech and prepared to travel to Jerusalem. As reported in Acts 19, he had gathered the Ephesian elders (the leaders) together to impart final words of wisdom and warning. The last piece of advice he offered before boarding his ship to leave Ephesus was this: *"And remember the words of the Lord Jesus, that He said, 'It is more blessed to give than to receive'"* (Acts 20:35). It is fitting that Paul singled out the leaders rather than the minions with the admonition to be selfless and generous. To whom much is given, much is required, indeed!

LEADERS ARE EXPECTED TO CONTROL THEIR ATTITUDE AND EMOTIONS, ESPECIALLY IN PUBLIC

Some leaders grow old but never grow up! They forever wear their emotions on their sleeves, engage in public tirades, and react hysterically and unpredictably to bad news. It is damaging enough for an organization to have an immature hothead work-ing in an entry-level position. As we learned in the passage from Luke, when this person is entrusted with more responsi-bility and privilege, a heightened level of behavior and integ-rity is required. The following story is one of THE BOOK's more powerful warnings of what happens when a leader loses it.

HEROD THE HORRENDOUS

Perhaps the most vicious act perpetuated by any biblical leader who lost emotional control was when Herod ordered the murder of the innocents, as reported in Matthew 2. Stung by a sense of betrayal after the wise men failed to return to him to disclose the location of the baby Jesus, Herod ordered his troops to murder every child two years of age and under in Bethlehem and its sur-rounding districts in an attempt to eliminate what he perceived as a threat to his throne. A side lesson to learn from this treachery is to never underestimate the impact that damaged pride can have on the morally ungrounded.

Herod's rash act of mass murder succeeded only in guarantee-ing him a hotter place throughout eternity, and it brings to life the words of the Psalmist who testifies to the futility of man trying to counteract God's will and ways—words that apply equally to those today who set themselves above God and attempt to derail His plans and purposes:

> Why do the nations rage, and the people plot a vain thing? The kings of the earth set themselves. And the rulers take counsel together, against the Lord and against His Anointed, saying, "Let us break Their bonds in pieces and cast away Their cords

from us." He who sits in the heaven shall laugh; The Lord shall hold them in derision. Then He shall speak to them in His wrath, and distress them in His deep displeasure: "Yet I have set My King on My holy hill of Zion." [Pss. 2:1–6]

Don't you love it? He who sits in heaven shall laugh! If only the faces behind the cultural forces I noted in the preface would realize their efforts against God and His people—you and me included—will ultimately fail! Until that day, we are commissioned to stay alert and contend for the faith and for our faith. Following God's mandate that leaders should be held more accountable is an idyllic and credible place for us to start, and not only in the workplace, but in our homes as well.

As you evaluate the leadership of your organization, it is essential that you detach yourself from sentimentalism and face reality about the effectiveness of your leaders. Tenure, credentials, and experience *do not* substitute for results. Thus, if you have any poorly performing leaders within your organization, do the following immediately: Sit down with them and redefine performance expectations, with an appropriate deadline and consequence for failing to succeed. Then help them devise a plan to reach the objectives. If they turn things around, you will have saved them. If they fail to reverse their downward spiral, even after you have so clearly outlined expectations and helped them plan for success, then you may very well save their subordinates or the organization overall by replacing them.

OMEGA

"And he [Jonah] said to them, 'Pick me up and throw me into the sea; and then the sea will become calm for you. For I know that this great tempest is because of me'" (Jon. 1:12).

1. As a leader, it is time for you to toughen up, tighten up, straighten up, grow up, and go up! Lead by personal example and not personal convenience. Commit yourself to a cause; do not commit the cause to yourself. Do not even think about raising the bar for others if your own bar is so low you keep tripping over it. Honestly assess and determine whether there are areas in which you have developed a sense of entitlement as a leader. What are they? Recognize them and repent.

2. Hire and promote leaders slowly, and fire bad ones quickly! There is too much at risk to allow pretenders with titles to play "amateur hour" with your culture, people, customers, brand, and future. Are you currently tolerating an ineffective leader in your organization? When will you stop working around the problem and deal with it?

"Woe to you, scribes and Pharisees, hypocrites! For you devour widows' houses, and for a pretense make long prayers. Therefore you will receive greater condemnation" (Matt. 23:14).

What Is the Most Effective Leadership Style?

MAN'S WISDOM AND WAY

Command and control is what works. You have to be able to control the environment and the people in it if you want to stay in power. Keep people on a short leash, and never let them forget who is in charge. Become indispensable by making all the decisions, solving all the problems, and coming up with every idea. Make sure your people understand that they are there to add value to you and keep you happy.

The classic, command-and-control management style ("My way or the highway," "Don't get out of that box," or "If I want your opinion, I'll give it to you") was dumb 30 years ago, but you could get away with it then because workers were less mobile and more loyal. We now live in the age of the free agent. Employees are much more willing to change jobs, cities, and careers than ever before. The new generation of workers also tends to be more spoiled, entitled, and pampered than those of us 50 and older could have ever dreamt possible back when we were working our way up through the ranks. Command-and-control management has always been ill advised. Today it is an invitation to leadership irrelevance. The bottom line: Your people are not there for you, you are there for them. You need them more than they need you. Your team is the center of your workplace universe; you are not!

THE BOOK's WISDOM AND WAY

The antithesis of a command-and-control leadership mind-set was described well by Paul: *"Let nothing be done through selfish ambition or conceit, but in lowliness of mind let each esteem others better than himself. Let each of you look out not only for his own interests, but also for the interests of others"* (Phil. 2:3–4).

Frankly, every Christian willing to face the corruption of his or her own heart—and who is painfully aware of his or her own inadequacies, weaknesses, sins, need for grace, mercy, and forgiveness—will find Paul's admonition to esteem others more highly than oneself a fairly simple and reasonable task.

In fact, how you regard others in the workplace, especially those subordinate to you, speaks volumes about the state of your heart and mind. If you see team members as mere tools to push and manipulate for the purpose of increasing your personal status, satisfaction and enrichment, and fail to realize that it is your responsibility to meet their needs and add value to them, then you are a tyrant, not a leader. And there is no ingredient more toxic to an organization than the command-and-control tyrant.

The opposite of command-and-control, tyrannical-style leadership is servant leadership. Despite old-school thinking, servant-leaders are not doormats, and servant leadership does not diminish your authority. The fact is that only the strong can serve, and being a servant-leader is the fastest and most credible method for increasing your leadership influence and shifting your culture from ho-hum to a category of one.

A SERVANT-LEADER'S JOB DESCRIPTION

Servant leadership is greatly misunderstood and grossly underestimated. In fact, when I begin to discuss servant leadership at workshops I am teaching, I can see some of the old-school types squirm a bit. They think that serving is "soft." They prefer to talk about "hard" numbers and fear that my class is going to be filled with warm and fuzzy, Pollyanna, happy hot tub talk!

The opposite end of the spectrum is represented well by a seminar attendee who once complained, "I like the idea of servant leadership. But I don't like the way some employees take advantage of it." When I asked how they take advantage, she replied, "They sit back and watch as I do their work for them."

Let me be clear: Doing the work for someone else while they watch you is not servant leadership, it is martyrdom!

While there may be occasions when a leader pitches in to do someone's work to help bail the team out of a busy moment, doing it regularly ensures inevitable team malfunctions and failures. In fact, coddling others in this manner creates entitled employees and exhausted leaders!

To help you gain a snapshot of what a servant-leader looks like in action, consider these 12 responsibilities that help comprise a servant-leader's job description.

29

1. Lead by example, with unquestionable character and consistent competence.
2. Set clear vision and expectations for followers.
3. Give honest feedback so that team members know where they stand and how to improve.
4. Train, coach, and mentor those you are responsible for to upgrade their skill levels and make them more valuable.
5. Keep your commitments, without excuses and regardless of the cost.
6. Show team members what good performance looks like, without doing their job for them!
7. Engage and listen to team members so that they feel understood.
8. Learn how to motivate everyone on your team as a unique individual.
9. Model the right attitude, integrity, and discipline. Be a walking example for the behaviors you value and expect to see in others.
10. Care enough to confront team members and hold them accountable when they are off track.
11. Positively reinforce team members; let them in on things; demonstrate appreciation for their contribution; and look for opportunities to build them up.
12. Give new opportunities, latitude, and discretion so each team member can stretch beyond his or her comfort zone and grow.

As you can see, servant leadership is not for sissies. Despite the weakness often associated with the word *servant*, serving effectively demands enormous strength.

Without a doubt, some people are easier to serve than others. This is because not everyone is equally likable and pleasant to be around. But servant-leaders do not have the luxury of picking and choosing who they will add value to. If someone is on your team, you are obliged to serve them. Jesus demonstrated this principle in John 13 when, knowing that Judas Iscariot would sell Him out that very evening, He washed his feet.

Did you also notice as you read the job description that the essence of servant leadership is to add value to others by meeting their needs? As you review it again, think about Jesus. How many of these tasks did He perform with His disciples? Think of specific examples. It will not take long to figure out that He was 12 for 12. Let us examine a couple of these occasions.

SERVING MEANS MEETING THE NEEDS OF OTHERS

Mark 10 describes how Jesus traveled through Jericho to Jerusalem during the final week of His life. There was plenty on His mind: for starters, His upcoming betrayal, trial, and crucifixion. But as He passed through the city He heard the cry of blind Bartimaeus importuning His aid, *"Jesus, Son of David, have mercy on me!"* (Mark 10:47). The crowd told blind Bart to quiet down, but he continued all the more. His persistence paid off! Bartimaeus garnered Jesus's attention—perhaps because this lowly, blind beggar recognized Jesus as the promised Messiah by referring to Him as the Son of David—at the very time the learned and privileged Pharisees almost unanimously rejected Him. While Bartimaeus lacked eyesight, the rulers conspiring to kill Jesus suffered from a blindness of the mind. At Jesus's call, and with his spiritual eyes opened to the possibility of a cure, Bartimaeus even cast aside his garment, lest it inhibit the speed of his response. The crowd that had, moments before, rebuked him now cheered him forward. Take a look at what happened next: *"So Jesus stood still and commanded him to be called. Then they called the blind man, saying to him, 'Be of good cheer. Rise, He is calling you.' And throwing aside his garment, he rose and came to Jesus. So Jesus answered and said to him, 'What do you want Me to do for you?'"* (Mark 10:49–51).

Those nine words uttered by Christ show servant leadership in its purest form: taking the time to set your own agenda aside to meet the needs of others because you fully understand that others *are* your agenda!

What is interesting about the timing of the Bartimaeus encounter is that it comes just a few verses after His disciples, John and James, in an attempt to leverage their joint influence, approached Jesus with a power-grab proposition to strengthen their personal leadership position. These "Sons of Thunder," members of Jesus's inner circle, asked that they be permitted to sit on the right- and left-hand side of Jesus in His kingdom. Ever the Master Teacher, Jesus did not expatiate upon their fault and point out that the selfishness of their request demonstrated their inadequacy and disqualified them for the posts. Instead, He recognized a teachable moment, responding to their ignorance and ambition with a stirring dissertation on how true greatness comes not from position, but through serving. His words were intended for the benefit of all 12 disciples, not just James and John, because the indignation demonstrated by the other 10 in response to the brothers' ploy proved that they themselves were as much motivated by ambition as James and John; they were as averse to surrender as the others were anxious to obtain the highest place of power. Thus, in the aftermath of the brothers' request, and just before entering Jericho to serve Bartimaeus, Jesus announced the entry price for greatness: *"You know that those who are considered rulers over the Gentiles lord it over them, and their great ones exercise authority over them. Yet it shall not be so among you; but whoever desires to become great among you shall be your servant. And whoever desires to be first, shall be a slave of all. For even the Son of Man did not come to be served, but to serve, and to give His life a ransom for many"* (Mark 10:43–45).

Jesus made clear that no one should seek power under the illusion that happiness consists of its possession, or that it would somehow make that individual superior to others. Rather, for Christian leaders to employ legitimate ambition, they must seek to use whatever power and position they have to advance God's agenda and augment the worth and welfare of their family, friends, teammates, and community.

Notice also that as the ultimate servant-leader, Jesus did not lecture James and John about servant leadership. He *showed* them what it looked like through his interaction with Bartimaeus. The takeaway lesson: Talking about what servant leadership looks like is *helpful*. But showing others what servant leadership looks like is *powerful*. This is because most people would rather see a sermon than hear one.

ARE YOU A SHEPHERD OR A HIRED GUN?

Jesus contrasted His care for His flock to those who were strictly in it for the money. He compared real leadership through shepherding to the "gun for hire" in John 10:12–14. The differences apply just as aptly today when you compare servant-leaders, who give themselves to meet the needs of their teams, to the pretenders with titles who see their people strictly as the means to a selfish end. *"I am the good shepherd. The good shepherd gives His life for the sheep. But a hireling, he who is not the shepherd, one who does not own the sheep, sees the wolf coming and leaves the sheep and flees; and the wolf catches the sheep and scatters them. The hireling flees because he is a hireling and does not care about the sheep"* (John 10:12–14).

Hirelings are out for themselves. As soon as things get tough, they bail out on the sheep and shift into self-preservation mode.

Hirelings take no ownership over the development of their sheep. At best, they maintain them. Hirelings in leadership are the most scandalous sorts of impostors, engaging in narcissism while they neglect their flocks.

Moses and David were ideal candidates to lead their people because they had cut their teeth in the trenches of shepherding. In fact, David was the master shepherd of Israel. We see from his life that feeding sheep involves far more than just leading them to food. David rescued sheep from the mouth of both a lion and a bear and gave them reassurance and comfort when needed (see 1 Samuel 17:34 and Psalm 23:4). This is the kind of shepherding that fathers are supposed to do for their children and business leaders for those under their care.

Jesus, our Chief Shepherd, identified four major characteristics of a good shepherd:

1. First, the good shepherd personally knows his sheep: *"... he calleth his own sheep by name ..."* (John 10:3). In Bible times, shepherds would often give names to the sheep for which they were responsible. As they took care of their sheep, shepherds would become well acquainted with the unique characteristics and habits of each sheep. We should spend time with each person for whom we are responsible in order to discover his or her individual needs.

2. The second characteristic of a good shepherd is his leadership of the sheep: *"And when he putteth forth his own sheep, he goeth before them, and the sheep follow him ..."* (John 10:4). Shepherds not only lead their sheep to rich pastures, they also examine and prepare the fields to make sure there are no poisonous plants that could harm their sheep. In the same way, we are to disciple those under our care by teaching them biblical principles and protect them from wrong

34

doctrine, bad habits, and harmful activities that would degrade and deplete them.

3. Third, good shepherds set aside their personal goals in order to care for the sheep: *"... I lay down my life for the sheep"* (John 10:15). The Lord Jesus laid down His life for us, and we must be willing to lay down our lives for those He has placed under our care. This means that we must place the needs of our sheep ahead of our own plans and priorities (Gothard 2005).

   Paul explained this well in his letter to the Thessalonians when he reminded them that he esteemed them so much that he did not stop at imparting knowledge to them, but also gave *himself* for them, the essence of true servant leadership. *"So, affectionately longing for you, we were well pleased to impart to you not only the gospel of God, but also our own lives, because you had become dear to us"* (1 Thess. 2:8).

4. Finally, shepherds demonstrate concern for the physical and spiritual protection of their flocks in all areas of their life, not just while they are "on the clock." Consider the following words from Ezekiel. He could just as easily be speaking to any number of contemporary politicians, preachers, or business executives sent to prison for taking their hireling habits to corrupt extremes.

> And the word of the Lord came to me, saying, "Son of man, prophesy against the shepherds of Israel, prophesy and say to them, 'Thus says the Lord God to the shepherds: Woe to the shepherds of Israel who feed themselves! Should not the shepherds feed the flock? You eat the fat and clothe yourselves with the wool; you slaughter the fatlings, but you do not feed the flock. The weak you have not strengthened, nor have you healed those who were

sick, nor bound up the broken, nor brought back
what was driven away, nor sought what was lost; but
with force and cruelty you have ruled them. . . . '"
[Ezek. 32:2–4]

CHARACTERISTICS OF A HIRELING — THE HIRED GUN

In contrast to servant-leaders who care for and shepherd each
member of their team, a hireling is burdened and weakened by the
following characteristics:

- Hirelings value money and position more than they value
  people.
- Hirelings see their role as an opportunity for self-service
  rather than as a pathway to serving Christ by adding value to
  and meeting the needs of His flock.
- Because hirelings are selfish and proud; they are easy prey
  for Satan's temptations, readily sacrificing what is right for
  what is easy, cheap, popular, or convenient.
- Even at best, hirelings are concerned only with a team member's well-being and production while at work, divorcing concern for the flock's welfare outside the organization's walls.

THE RECIPE FOR GREATNESS

In the Gospels, there are numerous instances where the disciples
argue about greatness. This begs the question, is it wrong to aspire
to be great? Good question. Fortunately, Jesus settled this issue
long ago when He caught the 12 disciples disputing, yet again,
which one of them would be the greatest. Notice what He did
say — and what He did not say — about greatness in this instance:

"Then He came to Capernaum. And when He was in the house He asked them, 'What was it you disputed among yourselves on the road?' But they kept silent, for on the road they had disputed among themselves who would be the greatest. And He sat down, called the Twelve, and said to them, 'If anyone desires to be first, he shall be last of all and servant of all'" (Mark 9:33–35).

Did you catch it? Jesus never told His disciples any of the following:

1. Do not try to be great.
2. It is wrong to want to become great.
3. Being great is not important.

Instead, He offered a *recipe* for greatness: "to be last of all, a servant of all." You can rest assured that the recipe for true greatness has not changed over time.

JOHN MAXWELL, THE LEADER, THE CELEBRITY, THE SERVANT

My wife, daughter, and I traveled to Israel with members of the Christ Fellowship Church, located in West Palm Gardens, Florida. My longtime friend, leadership guru, and best-selling author, John Maxwell, along with his wife Margaret, cohosted the trip with the Mullins family, who do an outstanding job of leading Christ Fellowship Church.

John was one of the leaders of the tour; he was the celebrity, but he was also the servant. Everywhere we visited, John gave a small lesson to add insight and value to our experience. On the Mount of Beatitudes, he preached a moving sermon about the Sermon on the Mount. As we boated across the Sea of Galilee, John shared insight that placed us in the boat with the disciples the night Jesus walked to them on the water. On the Mount of Olives, John shared Scripture that put us in Jesus's sandals as He wept over Jerusalem. While on the Mount of Olives, John even performed a hilarious rap and dance, "Baal Busters," reenergizing the tired tour group and making him even more approachable. He then led us down a path to the Garden of Gethsemane, where we partook of a Communion that brought tears to the eyes of many.

At Caesarea, John gathered us in the ancient Roman Theater and brought to life Paul's bold defense there before King Agrippa. After this lesson, he invited anyone who wanted to talk more about Jesus and faith to visit with him. Following a rain shower at Beth Shen, while everyone else was standing in line for food, it was John who took his handkerchief and dried off the chairs the group would be using for lunch. Even with a nonstop schedule, John took the time to meet personal needs. He prayed one-on-one with whomever asked. Many times, despite the frantic pace and bustling crowds, I saw him, arm wrapped around the shoulder of another, walking, listening, conversing, and encouraging. He tirelessly posed for hundreds of photographs with group members at each stop. John even bought ice cream and other goodies for the entire bus, adding life, love, and laughter as we sojourned for nine days across Israel.

John was one of the tour's leaders, its biggest celebrity, and its most noble servant. Of the many priceless memories and lessons my family and I took away from our pilgrimage to Israel, John Maxwell's real-life lessons on how to be a servant-leader were the most valuable—and remain the most memorable.

I close out this chapter on the most effective leadership style with four questions to challenge your ego and motives:

1. Do you value people enough to add value to people?
2. Do you stoop to serve before you stand to lead?

3. Are you willing to decrease so that your people can increase?
4. Will you subordinate your own comfort and convenience to what's best for the team?

OMEGA

"He has shown you, O man, what is good; And what does the Lord require of you but to do justly, to love mercy, and to walk humbly with your God" (Mic. 6:8).

1. Based on the 12 criteria given, how do you rate as a servant-leader? Would your team say that your leadership style tends toward the tyrannical or toward the servant style? Which actions must you more consistently employ to become a more effective servant-leader?
2. Do you walk slowly through your workplace? Do you look for opportunities to connect with people, listen to them, engage them, and then find ways to add value to them by meeting their needs?

"For I have given you an example, that you should do as I have done to you" (John 13:15).

How Do I Recruit Great People?

The next three chapters cover recruiting, interview strategy, interview questions, and techniques. Even if you do not recruit or hire in your present job position, you should carefully study these chapters for two reasons:

1. What you learn will help you to add value to, and positively influence, those in your organization who do hire. This will edify your own worth within the organization.
2. There may come a day when hiring is part of your job description, and you will already be well prepared for this important responsibility.

MAN'S WISDOM AND WAY

With everything else we have to do on a daily basis, it's senseless to spend time recruiting until we need someone. When that time comes, we'll place an impressive ad in the paper that sizzles with opportunity and benefits. Then we'll hire someone with plenty of experience whom we all like.

Here are four facts concerning the four points in the preceding paragraph:

1. Recruiting should be a proactive discipline, because as desperation rises, standards fall.
2. Standard employment ads typically attract the bottom 30 percent of performers. To increase the quality of job candidates responding to a newspaper ad, it should be worded in a way that attracts people looking for opportunities rather than paychecks.
3. Past performance is a better indicator of future performance than is past experience.
4. Liking someone is no guarantee that he or she will get the job done. The world is filled with plenty of likable workplace laggards with neither the character nor competence necessary to add value to your organization. On the other hand, employees with solid character and competence tend to become far more likable over time, even if they don't bowl you over with a dynamic personality during the interview process.

THE BOOK'S WISDOM AND WAY

Hire for heart, attitude, and talent; train for skills and knowledge. The 12 men Jesus recruited as His disciples were not the most educated, experienced, or pedigreed candidates in the religion talent pool of their day. In the time of Jesus, men aspiring to greater religious enlightenment sought out rabbis and petitioned them, hoping to be accepted to study under their tutelage. The rabbis would accept only those whom they considered to have the highest potential for growth. The fact that the men Jesus chose for His team were not then studying under any such guru is evidence they were not considered to be "first-teamers." That Jesus actually called them, rather than waiting to be sought by them, was diametric to the traditional student-teacher protocol and relationship.

As you study what transpired during the time Jesus was teaching and grooming His disciples, you cannot help but be struck with the realization that perhaps His greatest miracle was enduring this bunch right up to the night of His arrest, when they all abandoned Him on His way to the cross! In Mark 9:19, a frustrated Jesus asked these men how much longer He would have to put up with them! Yet no group of men ever turned the world upside down and changed it forever like this unique band of brothers.

What did Jesus see in these rough and raw men? It was not experience, education, social standing, or credentials. What He did see in the midst of their imperfections was a teachable and moldable spirit. While their character still fell far short of the ideal when Jesus recruited them, it was fundamentally strong enough to give Jesus a foundation of substance to build upon. He was then able to develop them through His example, Spirit, and mentorship and to mold them into the men their Creator intended for them to be.

Perhaps the greatest lesson Jesus taught us by selecting and developing this thickheaded horde is that, when we humble ourselves and remain teachable, He can use us to accomplish great things, despite our flaws, shortcomings, and failures. By putting the right person in an environment buttressed by clarity, inspiring

43

leadership, accountability, and a commitment to develop its human capital, you can do likewise with your own team members.

Hiring great people requires a solid strategy for both recruiting and interviewing. Since I have written two previous books that cover numerous specific recruiting strategies, *Up Your Business* (Wiley 2007), and *TKO Hiring* (Wiley 2007), I present only an overall and effectual recruiting philosophy in this chapter, without delving into the technical aspects I covered in those two works. In the subsequent two chapters, I build on the Bible's recruiting maxims, and follow up with an intensive game plan for conducting potent interviews.

Frankly, if you do not hire the right people, much of what you learn in any business book or seminar is rendered irrelevant. You simply cannot execute strategy or reach your vision without the right people. Training, coaching, and mentoring bring low returns when invested in those who give you little to work with in terms of talent, attitude, character, energy, or drive. Attempting to build a strong culture populated with corrupt or incompetent performers is an exercise in futility. If you have wondered why I would commit so much of this book to recruiting, interviewing, and hiring great people, now you know.

RECRUIT THOSE WHO ARE ALREADY EMPLOYED AND PRODUCTIVE!

I do not mean to sound unkind, but you are very unlikely to build a team of eagles in your organization if you endeavor to staff your organization from the ranks of the unemployed. While there is hidden talent in the available pool of nonworking people, you are advised to first focus on recruiting people who are already productive. While there are normally exceptions to every rule, here is a recruiting mandate to remember: You cannot build a great team around potential exceptions! Focus on the rule.

During my seminars, someone will normally whine out the classic "loser's limp" that there is a "shortage of talented people" in that particular city. After I gently remind the class that excuses are the DNA of underachievers, I encourage them with the news that there is no shortage of talented people in a particular area. Rather, the most productive, successful, and talented people are normally getting the job done for someone else. They are already working. They don't show up at your place, hat in hand, begging for work.

LEARN FROM THE PAST

Consider that the following biblical stars were all busy, working, or otherwise engaged with worthwhile activities when they were called into service or promoted to greater opportunities. There is not space to include all examples from the Bible, but this compilation offers a convincing case to recruit the currently employed and/or productive!

1. We may safely assume that God did not call Noah out of idleness to spend decades of hard work building the ark. After the flood, Noah engaged in agricultural pursuits.
2. Abraham was a successful rancher as God used him to father a nation.
3. Joseph's talents and performance preceded his promotion by Pharaoh.
4. Jacob acquired his wealth working for his father-in-law Laban.
5. Moses was a shepherd when he was called by God to lead His people out of Egypt.
6. Jethro, father-in-law and mentor of Moses, was a priest.

7. Joshua was assistant and right-hand man to Moses. He succeeded Moses as the leader of Israel and led his people to conquer the Promised Land.

8. Caleb's high-performance track record prompted Joshua to honor his request and grant him Hebron.

9. Deborah was the judge of Israel when she went with Barak to defeat Sisera and his army.

10. Gideon was secretly threshing wheat in a wine press when the angel called him.

11. Ruth was working in the fields when discovered by Boaz.

12. Eli, Samuel's mentor, was a priest.

13. Samuel ministered before the Lord, even as a child.

14. David was tending sheep in the field when Samuel came to his father's house with the purpose of anointing the future king of Israel. He was the only one of the eight brothers Samuel evaluated who was engaged in work when Samuel came to call.

15. Elisha was plowing with 12 yoke of oxen before him when he was discovered and called by Elijah.

16. Ezra, a scribe who led the Jews in their return from Babylonian captivity to Israel, is thought to have written four biblical books: 1 and 2 Chronicles, Ezra, and Nehemiah.

17. Nehemiah was working as the cupbearer for King Artaxerxes when commissioned with his assignment to rebuild the wall of Jerusalem.

18. Esther was queen when she intervened with the king to save the Jews from Haman's plot.

19. Job, a successful rancher when used by God to smite Satan, has inspired men and women throughout the millennia.

20. Daniel had previously served other kings with excellence when Darius promoted him to a top position in his kingdom.

21. Amos was a sheep rancher when called to be God's prophet.
22. Zacharias, father of John the Baptist, was a priest.
23. Joseph, the earthly father chosen to raise Jesus, was a carpenter.
24. The Bethlehem shepherds were working the night shift, tending their flocks, when called by the angels to witness the newborn Christ.
25. Andrew, Peter, James, and John were all working as fishermen when called by Jesus.
26. The Samaritan woman used by Jesus to help bring revival to her village was preparing to draw water from a well when she encountered the Lord.
27. Matthew was working in a tax office when called by Jesus.
28. Stephen and Phillip (the evangelist) were working as servers in the new church when called to greater assignments.
29. Luke, the author of the Gospel bearing his name and Acts, was a doctor.
30. Paul was tirelessly working to persecute Christians when called to serve Christ.
31. Lydia, the first European convert, was a seller of purple. She and her household were baptized and hosted Paul and his traveling companions during his missionary journey to Philippi.
32. The eloquent and powerful Apollos was preaching at Ephesus when discovered by Aquila and Priscilla, who thereupon coached him to become an even greater spokesman for God.
33. Note the workers and laborers singled out and commended by Paul in his letter to the Romans, Chapter 16:
    - *"Greet Priscilla and Aquila, my fellow workers ..."* (Rom. 16:3).
    - *"Greet Mary, who labored much for us"* (Rom. 16:6).

- *"Greet Tryphena and Tryphosa, who have labored in the Lord"* (Rom. 16:12).
- *"Greet the beloved Persis, who labored much in the Lord"* (Rom. 16:12).
- *"Timothy, my fellow worker . . . greets you"* (Rom. 16:21).
- *"Gaius, my host, and the host of the whole church, greets you"* (Rom. 16:23).
- *"Erastus, the treasurer of the city greets you . . ."* (Rom. 16:23).

There is no pattern in the Scriptures of God using unproductive, lazy, or otherwise disengaged men or women in important endeavors.

You Need a Proactive Strategy!

In order to build a pipeline of talent that staffs current positions and fuels future growth, your organization must have a proactive recruiting strategy designed to attract passive job candidates into your organization. If you would like the short course for accomplishing this foremost task, read Chapter 1 ("Always Remember, It's the People, Stupid!") of my book *Up Your Business: 7 Steps to Fix, Build, or Stretch Your Organization* (Wiley 2007). A major benefit of developing a proactive hiring strategy is that it will keep you out of desperate situations where you are likely to lower standards just to hire a warm body to fill an empty position. Remember that hiring is a lot like dating: As desperation rises, standards fall!

In *Up Your Business*, I outline several key strategies for attracting high-quality, passive job candidates into your organization. Here is one rule: You will need to stop waiting to be hunted, and start hunting! You will also need to create a culture that becomes your number one recruiting tool. Your first step in this direction is taking better care of the great people you currently have working for you.

After all, how can you expect to attract eagles from other organizations if you are not taking care of the eagles you already have?

Shun the Laments of the Lazy

I would be remiss if I did not conclude this chapter on recruiting with a warning about, and an admonition to, the lazy. Isaac Newton's first law of motion states that objects in motion tend to remain in motion, and objects at rest tend to remain at rest. The same law applies to people. In an age of record-high unemployment, it is controversial to assert what I am getting ready to claim, but the sad truth is that many people do not have jobs because they do not want jobs. What is worse is their rationalization for *not* doing what is honorable and getting a job—any job—that would allow them to work as unto the Lord. Here are two common excuses, with my own corresponding interpretation. These truths will ruffle the feathers of those in denial, but I thank God that He long ago freed me from the bondage of trying to please people over Him.

1. **Lament of the lazy**: "I'm overqualified for the jobs that are available."

   Translation: "I'm proud, arrogant, and believe that there are certain jobs that are beneath me. I didn't go to college so that I could wait on tables, wash dishes, or become a salesperson. I'm less embarrassed by doing nothing and letting others take care of me than by engaging in honorable work that would rebuild my self-esteem and bring honor to God."

   "The lazy man says, 'There is a lion in the road! A fierce lion in the streets!' As a door turns on its hinges, so does the lazy man on his bed. The lazy man buries his hand in the bowl; it wearies

him to bring it back to his mouth. The lazy man is wiser in his own eyes than seven men who can answer sensibly" (Prov. 26:13–16).

2. **Lament of the lazy:** "I can make more money on unemployment than I can if I work at the jobs that are available. It doesn't make economic sense for me to work."

   Translation: "I'm just plain lazy and content being a leech that subtracts value from the productive members of society. I'm too shortsighted to see that by taking any available job, I could put myself in the path of meeting the right people or to avail myself of greater opportunities. I am content to do less than I can each day and, as a result, become less than I am as a human being. Besides, rationalizing, trivializing, and sanitizing my sloth sure beats breaking a sweat!"

   - *"The desire of the lazy man kills him, for his hands refuse to labor"* (Prov. 21:25).
   - *"And besides they learn to be idle, wandering about from house to house, and not only idle, but also gossips and busybodies, saying things which they ought not"* (1 Tim. 5:13).

The excuses for not working continue ad nauseam: "I could take that job, but it's not where I want to work." "It's not what I wish to do." "The hours are inconvenient." "That type of work makes me uncomfortable." Well, here is a wake-up call for those who engage in this sort of verbal vomit: That is precisely why work is called *work*! It is not always pleasant, easy, convenient, or about doing what you would like to do where you would like to do it! If work were intended to always be fun and filled with joy, you would be expected to pay admission each day just to enter into its glory!

As a Christian, you should be eager to help those who cannot work, but you should refuse to enable those who *will not* work.

50

In 2 Thessalonians 3:10, the apostle Paul writes, *"For even when we were with you, we commanded you this: If anyone will not work, neither shall he eat."*

Scriptures like these, and there are many, make it certain that indolence and idleness are accursed of God. Because of this, it is reasonable that those who choose to exempt themselves from work should also be deprived of food, the reward of labor. However, when Paul commanded that the willingly idle should not eat, he was not commanding that the lazy be forced to fast; rather, he forbade the Thessalonians from supplying them with food and thereby encouraging their indolence.

Theologian John Calvin noted in his commentaries on the Bible: "It should also be noted there are different ways of laboring. Whoever aids society by their industry, either by ruling his family, or by administering public or private affairs, or by counseling, or by teaching, or in any other way, is not to be reckoned among the idle. For Paul censures those lazy drones who live by the sweat of others, while they contribute no service in common for aiding the human race" (Calvin 2005, 355).

Speaking of work, proactive recruiting *is* work! Hard work! But you can either invest your energies into finding the right people and building a strong culture to retain them or invest those same energies in pushing the wrong people to do the right things. Frankly, since both methods require hard work, I am opting for the path that brings the payoff. How about you?

After following *How to Lead by THE BOOK*'s example of how to successfully recruit, there is still the important work of evaluating potential job candidates through the interview. The stakes are high for this important responsibility. Thus, the next chapter covers an interview strategy, and Chapter 6 provides interview questions to help you determine the applicant's character.

Omega

"Then Boaz said to his servant who was in charge of the reapers, 'Whose young woman is this?' So, the servant who was in charge of the reapers answered and said, 'it is the young Moabite woman who came back with Naomi from the country of Moab.' And she said, 'Please let me glean and gather after the reapers among the sheaves'" (Ruth 2:5–7).

1. What must you change about your recruiting strategy so that your efforts are focused on bringing into your organization the most productive job candidates, not the most desperate?
2. What about your environment would make it a compelling recruiting tool to attract top performers from other organizations? What can you do to improve it?

"And Jesus, walking by the Sea of Galilee, saw two brothers Simon called Peter, and Andrew his brother, casting a net into the sea; for they were fishermen. Then He said to them, 'Follow Me, and I will make you fishers of men'" (Matt. 4:18–19).

What Is the Best Interview Strategy?

MAN'S WISDOM AND WAY

Put job candidates at ease and then ask questions that determine their level of experience. Tell them all the great things about your company and, if they don't have any apparent major flaws, make them an offer. You don't want them to keep looking and take a job elsewhere. You have to make a fast hiring decision to take them out of the job market.

Hasty hiring brings eventual firing. And the financial and cultural damage the wrong employee inflicts upon your organization until his or her departure is staggering. Hire slowly and shrewdly. You are better off to be strategically short-staffed than foolishly "filled up."

When shorthanded, do not succumb to the temptation of lowering hiring standards to ease the barrier of entry to fill empty positions. Lowering your standards never pleases God. Do not look at unfilled positions throughout your organization as evidence that

God is not taking care of you, but rather as proof that He has something better planned for you.

"Though the fig tree may not blossom, nor the fruit be on the vines; though the labor of the olive may fail, and the fields yield no food; though the flock may be cut off from the fold, and there be no herd in the stalls — yet I will rejoice in the Lord, I will joy in the God of my salvation. The Lord God is my strength; He will make my feet like deer's feet, and He will make me walk on my high hills" (Hab. 3:17–19).

THE BOOK's WISDOM AND WAY

In Galatians 5:9, the apostle Paul warns, *"A little leaven leavens the whole lump."* He was speaking of the danger that a single iota of false teaching or vulgar values has to diminish the entire organization. First Corinthians 15:33 warns, *"Do not be deceived, evil company corrupts good habits."* These Scriptures are unmistakable in their admonition to carefully guard your personal and corporate associations.

In light of numerous biblical warnings against rubbing elbows with bad apples, it is essential that job interviews be rigorous in order to uncover undesirables and eliminate them from employment consideration before they are cashing your paychecks and staining your culture. There is too much at stake for you to hire quickly or recklessly: the value of your brand, team morale, organizational momentum, productivity, and your personal leadership credibility. It is also important to recognize that the easier you make it for someone to get a job, the less that person will appreciate it, respect it, and respect you. This is human nature: Whatever we gain too easily, we esteem too lightly. On the other hand, when you have to work hard to get a job, you appreciate it more and endeavor to rise to the expectations that come with it. For this reason, you are wise to follow the guidelines in this chapter for conducting interviews.

USE KNOCKOUT INTERVIEWS TO SCREEN OUT UNDESIRABLES AND SAVE TIME

Here is the challenge: You want to hire the right person, but you do not care to waste time visiting with unfit or derelict job candidates. What can you do?

Conduct a knockout interview before you ever meet such people. Even if they stop by in person to apply, you should review their application and resume and arrange to call them back to schedule an in-person interview before taking face time with them. The purpose of a knockout interview is to find a way to eliminate candidates from consideration before wasting time meeting with them. The knockout philosophy includes perusing the resumes and applications sent to you electronically or by mail and seeking reasons to jettison candidates from consideration. In an organization with high standards for excellence and a strong culture to protect, an applicant's inability to be faithful in little things (correctly spelled words, professional language, etc.) are reasons for disqualification from consideration. Knockout interviews help upgrade hiring from an inclusive process to an elimination process, thus saving your most valuable resource—*time*. To that end, knockout interviews are invaluable.

The questions you ask during a knockout phone interview are up to you and will depend on the nonnegotiables of the position for which you are hiring. You may want to ask applicants about whether they are available to work certain hours, a specific number of hours, or on specific days. If you need someone to work Saturdays and they cannot work Saturdays, why would you want to have them come to your office and waste both your time and their own to discover this?

We recently posted a job opening for an administrative assistant on a college web site where we have had prior success in hiring great people. Our e-mail box was overwhelmed with the volume of applications. Here is a rundown of how and why we were able to eliminate all but one candidate without squandering time in face-to-face meetings with unfit job candidates.

1. Some applicants had multiple spelling or grammatical errors on their e-mails or resumes. Knock out! (One of our corporate core values is attention to detail.)

2. Some sent e-mails in all-lowercase letters, as though they were writing a text message. Knock out!

3. An applicant failed to call back at the appointed time we had scheduled in reply to her resume. Knock out!

4. An applicant called one hour before the interview to cancel and move it to another day. Knock out!

5. While speaking with the applicant on the telephone, it was obvious that the she did not speak clearly or coherently. Knock out!

6. The applicant spelled his own last name wrong! He spelled it differently in two different places on the resume. Knock out!

There were others, but this is enough to support my example. We kept looking and found a great candidate who scored a +64 on the Anderson Hiring Profile, with no cautions or concerns. (An average score is a zero, with pluses or minuses indicating above or below job potential from there.) Throughout our hiring process for this position, he was the only candidate we actually spoke with at an in-person interview. The rest of the applicants were eliminated before they had a chance to waste our time and sap our productivity. Incidentally, this assistant's position was for a part-time worker, who will average around 15 hours per week. But we are unwilling to compromise our hiring standards at any level in our organization, because any weak link will affect the rest of the team.

Hiring is one of your most important responsibilities, and time is your most precious resource. You can address both of these issues by "firing before you hire," using a knockout process, either by phone or elimination criteria, as itemized in the preceding list.

If knockout interviews sound too harsh to you, or smack of lacking grace, please consider that what you owe the rest of the team is far more important than coddling and making excuses for an unprepared, careless, or unqualified person. Learn from the parable of the wise and foolish virgins taught by Jesus in Matthew 25:1–13. He shared this parable to emphasize the importance of being prepared when something you have been waiting for manifests. In the case of a job applicant, this "something" is a job opportunity.

> Then the kingdom of heaven shall be likened to ten virgins who took their lamps and went out to meet the bridegroom. Now five of them were wise, and five were foolish. Those who were foolish took their lamps and took no oil with them, but the wise took oil in their vessels with their lamps. But while the bridegroom was delayed, they all slumbered and slept. And at midnight a cry was heard. "Behold, the bridegroom is coming: go out to meet him." Then all those virgins arose and trimmed their lamps. And the foolish said to the wise, "Give us some of your oil, for our lamps are going out." But the wise answered, saying, "No, lest there should not be enough for us and you; but go rather to those who sell, and buy for yourselves." And while they went to buy, the bridegroom came,

and those who were ready went in with him to the
wedding, and the door was shut. Afterward the other
virgins came also, saying, "Lord, Lord, open to us!"
But he answered and said, "Assuredly, I say to you,
I do not know you." Watch therefore, for you know
neither the day nor the hour in which the Son of
Man is coming. [Matt. 25:1–13]

There are at least four applicable principles in this parable to support the proposition that a worthy candidate is obligated to be prepared for a job opportunity when it arises and that eliminating those who are not, through a knockout philosophy, is just and wise.

1. If you earnestly want something, your actions should demonstrate it by putting forth the forethought and effort necessary to get it. You must be prepared for the opportunity before it arises. After it arises, it is too late!

2. If you are unprepared for an opportunity when it arises, or if you otherwise botch it, you cannot expect to get a second chance, nor are you owed one. The door may close for good. In fact, any entity with high enough standards is not likely to allow someone another shot in this regard. An organization with a strong culture understands the peril of making excuses for people and giving them too much benefit of the doubt even *before* they hire them.

3. Those who are prepared and serious are under no obligation to bail out the unprepared from their unthinking, undisciplined sloth.

4. What was required to be successful was available to all 10 virgins. It was not kept as a secret or reserved for a select few. While all had equal access to what would make them successful, only five took the initiative to secure it. This initiative in itself is a powerful indicator of future performance.

Years ago I used to say, "We need to talk to a lot of people in order to find a great job candidate." Since then, I have changed my philosophy. Frankly, it is exhausting to speak to a lot of people if they are the wrong people! I now judge the strength of our interview process by how *few* folks we actually visit with face-to-face. Because of our knockout process, I am assured that the few who make the cut are much more likely to possess the right stuff.

Use Interviews as an Elimination Process

If a promising job candidate survives the knockout process, your work has only just begun. Your face-to-face interview should also be used as an attempt to eliminate that person and not as an exercise in inclusivity. To that end, you should *avoid* the following during an interview:

- Talking too much
- Using the forum as a time-wasting good-old-boy get-acquainted session
- Conducting the interview as though it were a casual conversation
- Degrading the interview into a sales pitch

During an interview, you should seek to determine a combination of character and competence traits that portend that the job candidate can contribute greatly to your organization. To determine these qualities, it is imperative to evaluate someone's past accomplishments. This is because past performance is a greater indicator of future performance than past experience. By digging deeply into someone's life, you can better determine if he or she has key traits like character, talent, attitude, energy, and drive. Critical success factors like these will show up in someone's life, and so will the lack of them. In other words, success leaves clues, and so does failure. Common sense tells us that if people were just average, or below, in their past five jobs, they are probably not going to change in the moving van on the way to your place.

Look Harder at Their Journey than Their Location

Throughout your interviews, do not judge applicants strictly by the station they have reached in life. Dig deeper and determine what they overcame to get there. The journey will tell you more about the strength of their character than their current location on life's ladder. This is because some people had a generous head start in life and took the freeway to their current status. Others took a toll road, filled with detours and potholes, but nonetheless persisted and, in the process, became stronger human beings than did the "silver spoon posse." After all, character strength is forged in the pit, not in the hammock. Proverbs tells us, *"For a righteous man may fall seven times and rise again, but the wicked shall fall by calamity"* (Prov. 24:16). This exercise is not designed to have you completely disregard people who had it easier in life. But it is only fair to assert that they have not yet faced the challenges, stress, stumbling blocks, or setbacks that would have given them the opportunity to forge character and develop the power of persistence and mental toughness so essential to success in any endeavor.

Let Your Light Dispel the Darkness

Since a key objective during your interview is to find a reason to say no to the job candidate, I recommend that you share your core values and other specific behavioral expectations with applicants *before you hire them.* Let them know that you have nonnegotiable standards for integrity, teamwork, attitude, attention to detail, and the like. Describe what these behaviors look like in practice, and share clear consequences you've laid out for those who do not live up to the standards. Applicants lacking these essential qualities will quickly become uncomfortable and probably decide to continue their job search elsewhere, to your great benefit.

There is a biblical principle at work supporting this strategy. The Bible says the following in John 3:20–21: *"For everyone practicing evil hates the light and does not come to the light, lest his deeds should be exposed. But he who does the truth comes to the light, that his deeds may be clearly seen, that they have been done in God."*

For instance, if one of your core values is teamwork, you might explain it this way: "John, I want to go over our company core values with you. I have them here in writing. You will notice that the first is 'teamwork.' In our organization, teamwork means that the good of the team comes before the personal comfort level or agenda of any one individual. In other words, lone wolves and selfish employees do not fit here. John, as I go over these other values with you, please understand that they are nonnegotiable behaviors in our organization. If you believe that you would have trouble working within these parameters, the time to let us know is now."

Frankly, many people are repelled by character-driven companies with high ethical standards and expectations, because they know it is only a matter of time before their selfishness, dishonesty, and moral corruption — their darkness — is discovered and exposed by your light. Aren't you better off to scare these folks away before they are on your payroll, lowering morale, mistreating customers and coworkers, and destroying your culture and leadership credibility? Remember, the best time to fire is before you hire!

In Chapter 9, I present five sample core values and discuss how to use them as a filter for hiring and firing.

Effective interviewing requires a serious strategy, high standards, and consistency. You must hire with your head and not with your heart. By embracing and applying the concepts presented in this chapter, you will serve as a sentry for your organization, protecting and preserving your culture, other team members, customers, your brand, morale, momentum, productivity, and personal credibility.

Whereas this chapter has presented a solid interview philosophy and strategy, Chapter 6 digs deeper and provides specific interview questions and guidelines to enhance and support this approach.

OMEGA

"Now at the end of the days, when the king had said that they should be brought in, the chief of the eunuchs brought them in before Nebuchadnezzar. Then the king interviewed them, and among them all none was found like Daniel, Hananiah, Mishael, and Azariah; therefore they served before the king. And in all matters of wisdom and understanding about which the king examined them, he found them ten times better than all the magicians and astrologers who were in all his realm. Thus Daniel continued until the first year of King Cyrus" (Dan. 1:18–21).

1. What can you do to turn your interviews into an elimination process? Be specific.
2. What criteria can you begin using to knock out unqualified, unprepared, or undesirable candidates before you personally interview them?

"To the pure all things are pure, but to those who are defined and unbelieving, nothing is pure; but even their mind and conscience are defiled. They profess to know God, but in works they deny Him, being abominable, disobedient, and disqualified for every good work" (Titus 1:15–16).

CHALLENGE 6

What Are the Best Interview Questions to Ask?

MAN'S WISDOM AND WAY

Ask job applicants about their strengths and weaknesses, and have them explain their experience level and credentials. Don't come on too strong or you might scare off a good candidate. When all is said and done, go with what your gut tells you.

Your gut is not a reliable barometer of a candidate's character and competence. You are as likely to hire an eagle using crystal balls and mediums as you are through the wisdom of your gut. Remember, your gut is a garbage dump! Using it to hire can reduce your culture into much of the same.

THE BOOK's Wisdom and Way

In Matthew 23, Jesus lit into the scribes and Pharisees with a pointed and powerful diatribe, announcing seven woes against them. Here is an excerpt: *"Woe to you, scribes and Pharisees, hypocrites! For you cleanse the outside of the cup and dish, but inside they are full of extortion and self-indulgence. Blind Pharisee, first cleanse the inside of the cup and dish, that the outside of them may be clean also"* (Matt. 23:25).

This metaphor reminds us that the outside of a person can be quite deceiving. Rarely is this truer than when you evaluate a candidate during a job interview. You hire someone who looks the part, only to learn later that there is often a significant difference between appearance and performance. The quality of your hiring decisions is ultimately determined by how proficient you are at uncovering the "inside of the cup."

The best way to determine the inside of an applicant's cup is to delve into his or her life history. By asking job candidates a series of competence- and character-determining questions, you will get a highly accurate assessment of their moral and tactical strengths and weaknesses. The preparation required to structure an interview in this fashion greatly lessens the chances you will be duped by their facade, and minimizes the chances that you will compound the error by asking weak questions for which they have canned, panned, and polished answers prepared.

Ask unexpected questions, as you will never get a truer glimpse of people's character than when you catch them unprepared. Consider the words of Christian author C. S. Lewis: "If there are rats in a cellar, you are most likely to see them if you go in very suddenly. The suddenness of your approach doesn't create the rats; it only prevents them from hiding" (Lewis 2001, 192).

When you ask a sudden, unexpected, somewhat stressful question during an interview, you do not *create* a defensive, immature, irritable person. You merely *reveal* the defensive, immature, irritable person seated before you.

WHY HIRING RIGHT IS THE KEY

This is the third consecutive chapter in this book that concerns an aspect of hiring. Why all the fuss about getting the right people? Let me reiterate what I stated in Chapter 4: Without the right people, the rest of what I present in this book will not help you much. For instance, consider how futile it is to discuss these organizational topics if you do not have great people in place.

1. *Vision*. How does it benefit you to have bold vision if you do not have people capable of taking you there? After all, a great dream with the wrong team is a nightmare!
2. *Training*. What good does it do to train people who lack drive, character, or talent? Taking stronger whips to dead horses will not move them! *"Do not speak in the hearing of a fool. For he will despise the wisdom of your words"* (Prov. 23:9).
3. *Strategy*. Can you think of a more colossal waste of time than devising an "A" strategy and asking "C" players to execute it? Watching this in action would be comical if it were not so utterly pathetic!

Hiring right makes accomplishing the rest of your business objectives more obtainable. Hiring recklessly renders your organizational aspirations irrelevant. You must hire men and women who have capacity to do more than just get by. They must be able to excel in their work: *"Do you see a man who excels in his work? He will stand before kings; he will not stand before unknown men"* (Prov. 22:29).

SEVEN TRAITS AND FIFTEEN QUESTIONS

Character is commonly defined as "the combination of qualities or features that distinguishes one person, group, or thing from another." Thus, character is one's moral code.

Integrity, on the other hand, is defined as "firm adherence to a code of especially moral or artistic values." In other words, character is one's moral code, and integrity means that you live in strict adherence to that code. This is precisely why right character must precede integrity.

If someone's moral code says that it is acceptable or desirable to take hostages, burn crosses in someone's yard, blow up buildings, or otherwise injure innocent people in order to achieve an end, and this person acts in accordance with that code, by definition he or she is living with integrity. For this reason, effective interviews must focus on cracking the code of job applicants, then examining their life to determine whether they have lived in alignment with that code—if they have lived with integrity.

Following are seven key character traits to look for during the interview process that help you to crack the code. Along with them, I have included 15 related questions you can ask to help determine these characteristics. Change the words to fit your own style and personality. You should also ask competence-based questions, which can be found in Chapter 1 of my book, *Up Your Business: 7 Steps to Fix, Build, or Stretch Your Organization* (Wiley 2007). The purpose of this chapter is to devise an interview strategy that focuses on determining character.

For starters, it is helpful to assemble a checklist of character traits that are most important to you and then fashion questions to help determine those qualities. Use those I provide as a starting point. A sound interview strategy mandates that after you

66

receive an answer to an interview question, you must follow up with deeper-probing questions to gain a clearer understanding of the applicant and his or her abilities.

Probing questions are simple inquiries that demand more specificity. Here are some examples.

"How did you accomplish that?"
"What did you learn?"
"Why would you say that?"
"What mistakes did you make that you would fix if you did it all over again?"
"Describe the biggest decision you made to get that result."
"What were the three toughest changes you had to make to get from where you were to where you are?"
"Explain resistance you had to overcome and how you did it."

You will weed out exaggeration to get a glimpse of the candidate's true nature as you follow up your initial questions with more probing ones.

Remember, you can teach skills and knowledge, but you cannot teach character! As reported in Acts 6:5, when the disciples chose seven key men to assist in the growing church's duties, *"And they chose Stephen, a man full of faith and the Holy Spirit."* Prior to their selection process, the criteria they established for the new recruits was this: *"Therefore brethren, seek out from among you seven men of good reputation, full of the Holy Spirit and wisdom, whom we may appoint over this business . . ."* (Acts 6:3).

The apostles set a clear and powerful example with their established criteria: Character counts! Hire it in! Following are the seven key traits to look for with accompanying questions to help you determine the moral soundness of job applicants. I have also included a supporting Scripture that underscores the importance of each trait.

SEVEN CHARACTER TRAITS AND RELATED INTERVIEW QUESTIONS

1. **Character trait: truthfulness.** *"Therefore, putting away all lying, let each one of you speak truth with his neighbor, for we are members of one another"* (Eph. 4:25).

   Is there anything wrong with telling a caller, vendor, or someone asking for a contribution that someone is not in, even if he or she is?

   Has a former boss ever asked you to tell a white lie? How did you handle it?

2. **Character trait: work ethic.** *"And whoever compels you to go one mile, go with him two"* (Matt. 5:41).

   Could you define for me what you believe doing a good job is? A great job?

   In your last position, what particular task or project do you believe you did a great job with? Be specific. Explain why you feel it was great.

3. **Character trait: teachability.** *"And Jesus increased in wisdom and stature, and in favor with God and men"* (Luke 2:52).

   Please name for me some of the books, CDs, or DVDs you have in your personal development library at home?

   What is the last serious book you read? What did you like best about it? What have you applied or changed as a result of reading it?

4. **Character trait: keeping commitments.** *"But I say to you that for every idle word men may speak, they will give account of it in the day of judgment"* (Matt. 12:36).

   Under what circumstances is it acceptable to not keep a commitment or to not do what you said you would do?

   What is the last commitment you failed to keep? Why?

5. **Character trait: a forgiving spirit.** *"For if you forgive men their trespasses, your heavenly Father will also forgive you"* (Matt. 6:14).

   What is the hardest thing you have had to forgive in the workplace?

   How did you handle it? Are you still dealing with it?

6. **Character trait: timeliness and meeting deadlines.** *"If a man makes a vow to the Lord, or swears an oath to bind himself by some agreement, he shall not break his word; he shall do according to all that proceeds out of his mouth"* (Num. 30:2).

   When was the last time you were late to anything? Why? How late were you? How did you handle it?

   Here is a famous quote: "Being late is the arrogant choice." Do you agree, or do you feel it is too harsh and judgmental? Do you believe that being late is a sign of arrogance?

   Have you ever missed a work-related deadline? Tell me about it.

7. **Character trait: acceptance of responsibility.** *"So David said to God, 'I have sinned greatly, because I have done this thing; but now, I pray, take away the iniquity of Your servant, for I have done very foolishly'"* (1 Chron. 21:8).

   You have obviously accomplished a lot in your life; if you had to list three factors that have prevented you from being even further along than you are now, what are they? [Note: Do your interviewees accept responsibility by blaming their own internal decisions, or do they shift blame to outside conditions?]

   We expect anyone working for us to take some risks, seize the initiative, and make mistakes from time to time. Describe for me some of the bigger mistakes you have made in past jobs and what you learned from them.

RAISE THE BAR AND EXPAND YOUR LIST

I encourage you to expand the list of seven key traits to cover other moral qualities necessary to meet your expectations, align with your values, and anchor integrity into your culture. In 1 Timothy 3:1–7, the apostle Paul lays out 15 specific traits to seek when selecting church leaders. His criteria applies equally well to leaders of all organizations. Consider how you can weave Paul's 15 criteria from that passage into your hiring standards to help you with your personnel selection process:

1. "Above reproach." If someone brought charges against this person, everyone would laugh at him!
2. "The husband of but one wife." This does not mean "married only once," but rather "totally faithful."
3. "Temperate." This clearheaded individual doesn't make impulsive decisions.
4. "Self-controlled." This person does not spontaneously say or do foolish things.
5. "Respectable." You can count on this person to conduct him- or herself in an honorable manner and to live an orderly life.
6. "Hospitable." This person loves people and will make strong connections with other employees, vendors, and customers.
7. "Able to teach." The good leader may not be the most talkative. He or she is the one who exhibits the deepest understanding of moral principles and their application to one's personal and business life.
8. "Not given too much wine." Shun the partiers who put themselves in compromising situations where they are given to poor judgment, loose speech, and regrettable behavior.

9. "Not violent." Avoid the too-competitive person who is always out to win at any cost, without regard to your values, culture, reputation, and people.
10. "Gentle." This leader may hate a performance, but still loves the performer. He or she is more of a coach than a cop and is persuasive without being abrasive.
11. "Not quarrelsome." Avoid the contentious individual always ready to fight or to pick a fight. Generally motivated by pride or self-seeking, this person is more interested in being right than in having strong relationships.
12. "Not a lover of money." Love of possessions ultimately destroys love of people. And people must be the Christian leader's priority.
13. "Manages his or her own family well." Our ability to influence others for good is seen first in the family. If people cannot lead their families well, how fit are they to lead your business and people?
14. "Not be a recent convert." You can tell the kind of fruit a plant produces only after it has matured. Do not move someone into leadership before he or she has developed the character traits necessary for effective and moral performance.
15. "A good reputation with outsiders." Men and women of good reputation outside of your organization are quick to recognize phonies.

A general rule I follow is to not hire or promote those who ache for leadership. Rather, I hire and promote those who yearn to become the kind of person an effective leader must be. Determining key character traits with questions like these will help you discern whether you have such a person before you during an interview.

JESUS INTERVIEWS THE RICH, YOUNG RULER

Matthew, Mark, and Luke all report on Jesus's encounter with the rich, young, ruler. It was a tough interview. What is striking is that Jesus does not try very hard to win him over, despite the young man's earnestness. This was the one, and perhaps only, person who came to Jesus but was not saved. Here is what happened:

> Now behold, one came and said to Him, "Good Teacher, what good thing shall I do that I may have eternal life?" So He said to him, "Why do you call Me good? No one is good but One, that is God. But if you want to enter into life, keep the commandments." He said to Him, "Which ones?" Jesus said, "You shall not murder, You shall not commit adultery, You shall not steal, You shall not bear false witness, Honor your father and mother, and, You shall love your neighbor as yourself." The young man said to Him, "All these things I have kept from my youth. What do I still lack?" Jesus said to him, "If you want to be perfect, go, sell what you have and give to the poor, and you will have treasure in heaven; and come, follow Me." But when the young man heard that saying, he went away sorrowful, for he had great possessions. [Matt. 19:16–22]

To fully grasp all that was going on in this short encounter, these few verses warrant far deeper scrutiny than a first read or glance can provide. Following is a dissection and analysis of each sentence. See how many helpful lessons you can extract:

"Now behold, one came and said to Him, 'Good Teacher, what good thing shall I do that I may have eternal life?'"

The rich man approached Jesus with respect, despite His ordinary appearance. He asked a good question, demonstrating that he believed in eternal life. The rich are apt to think it below them to ask such a question, and young people think they have time enough not to be concerned. In this type of encounter today, most evangelicals would put on their hard sell and offer a three-step presentation of the Gospel, asking for a commitment to Christ. Jesus did nothing of the kind.

"So He said to Him, 'Why do you call Me good? No one is good but One, that is God. But if you want to enter into life, keep the commandments.' He said to Him, 'Which ones?' Jesus said, 'You shall not murder, You shall not commit adultery, You shall not steal, You shall not bear false witness, Honor your father and mother; and, You shall love your neighbor as yourself.'"

Jesus challenged him a bit on his notion of what is truly good and then reminded him of God's written law. In listing these commandments, Jesus referred to the sixth, seventh, eighth, ninth, and fifth commandments of Exodus 20, in that order, deliberately skipping over the tenth commandment and going directly to Leviticus 19:18: *"You shall love your neighbor as yourself."* The commandments from Exodus 20 were from the second tablet, those relating to one's relationship with others. Jesus's reply was probing—a test of sorts—seeking to determine the man's state of heart.

"The young man said to Him, 'All these things I have kept from my youth. What do I still lack? Jesus said to him, 'If you want to be perfect, go, sell what you have and give to the poor, and you will have treasure in heaven; and come, follow Me.'"

Jesus did not dispute the man's self-righteous claim to have always obeyed the commandments listed. Rather, He focused on making a more vital point. By giving the order to sell his possessions and follow Him, He was asking two things from this man:

1. That he obey the commandments of the first tablet, which relate to man's relationship with God, specifically the admonition that one would not put any idols (in this case, his riches) ahead of God. In addition, Jesus implicitly returned to the tenth commandment He had earlier skipped, *"Thou shall not covet,"* knowing it was this man's specific problem. The rich man coveted his own possessions. By telling him to sell them, Jesus broke down the man's self-righteousness and exposed the poverty of his heart. The rich ruler could have repented, embraced faith in Christ, and thus would been saved. Instead, he embraced his trust in possessions and walked away.

2. Jesus's invitation to the man to sell his possessions and *"come, follow Me"* tested the man's faith and belief in Christ, a prerequisite for him to attain eternal life. Jesus's request was not unreasonable. After all, from whom had the ruler received the wealth? Didn't God have a right to recall what he had only lent? Did this fellow have any right to complain if God, who had temporarily elevated him above the masses, should afterward reduce him to a level equal with them? Didn't God have as much right to disperse his wealth among the poor as He had earlier to bestow it upon one single man? Besides, when the sacrifice he was asked to make would contribute so much to the comfort of others, and when it would ultimately offer him a rich return, could Jesus's request in any way be deemed unreasonable (Simeon 1955, 94)? Jesus set

the bar high during his interview, and it was the applicant's job to stretch to reach it. It was not the obligation of Jesus to lower the bar to accommodate the man's comfort level.

"But when the young man heard that saying, he went away sorrowful, for he had great possessions."

The ruler had an inclination to Christ, and thus was loath to part ways with Him. But he left, sorrowfully, embracing the status quo, reaffirming his independent spirit, but failing the interview.

Jesus was not, and is not, interested in lukewarm followers — pretenders who confess Him with their mouths but deny them with their lifestyles. He established a standard during the interview and the rich man failed to meet it. Jesus did not beg, plead, lower the bar or sweeten the deal in an effort to cajole the rich man aboard his team. Instead, the interview was an elimination process, just as yours must be.

TWO REMINDERS FROM *HOW TO RUN YOUR BUSINESS BY THE BOOK*

Two key hiring strategies I included in *How to Run Your Business by THE BOOK* (Wiley 2009), bear repeating here:

1. *Pray before you hire.* Follow the example of Jesus before He chose the 12 disciples: Pray! Pray that God sends you the right people and that He grants you discernment during the interview.

2. *Do not get blown away by personal appearance!* Making emotional decisions during interviews based on prejudices, stereotypes, and personal appearances is one of the most common hiring errors. Remember the words of God to Samuel as he

was evaluating Jesse's eight sons in His quest to discover who to anoint as king. Samuel was blown away by the king-like appearance of Eliab: *"So it was, when they came, that he looked at Eliab and said, 'Surely the Lord's anointed is before Him!' But the Lord said to Samuel, 'Do not look at his appearance or at his physical stature, because I have refused him. For the Lord does not see as man sees: for man looks at the outward appearance, but the Lord looks at the heart'"* (1 Sam. 16:6–7). History goes on to show that Eliab was far too petty and selfish to have been a great king.

It also helps to remember that one chapter before Samuel's encounter with Eliab, he anointed Saul as Israel's first king. Saul was an abject failure as king. But take a look at how his physical appearance is described: *"And he had a choice and handsome son whose name was Saul. There was not a more handsome person than he among the children of Israel. From his shoulders upward he was taller than any of the people"* (1 Sam. 9:2).

How many Sauls have you seen during your career—or perhaps even hired because they had the right look—only to discover later that their style disguised the sad fact that they lacked substance? Endeavor to see job candidates during an interview as God sees them: from the inside of the cup out. Look at their hearts, and hire with your head!

OMEGA

"Then they lifted up their voices and wept again; and Orpha kissed her mother-in-law, but Ruth clung to her. And she said, 'Look, your sister-in-law has gone back to her people and to her gods; return after your sister-in-law.' But Ruth said: 'Entreat me not to leave you, or to turn back from following after you; for wherever you go, I will go; and wherever you lodge, I will lodge; your people shall be my people, and your God my God. Where you die, I will die, and there will I be buried. The Lord do so to me, and more also, if anything but death parts you and me'" (Ruth 1:14–17).

1. What do you now recognize as your chief interviewing flaw?
2. What other character traits do you want to dig for during an interview? Which questions can you ask to help you achieve that end?

"This you know, that all those in Asia have turned away from me, among whom are Phygellus and Hermogenes. The Lord grant mercy to the household of Onesiphorus, for he often refreshed me, and was not ashamed of my chain; but when he arrived in Rome, he sought me out very zealously and found me. The Lord grant to him that he may find mercy from the Lord in that Day—and you know very well how many ways he ministered to me at Ephesus" (2 Tim. 1:15–18).

What Is the Most Productive Way to Give Feedback?

MAN'S WISDOM AND WAY

You have to be careful with feedback. If you pat people on the back, it can make them lazy. At the same time, if you get in their face about performance shortfalls, they only get worse or poison the culture by complaining to others about how badly you treat them. Overall, it's best to play feedback close to the vest. You get more out of people if you keep them a bit off balance.

If ignorance is truly bliss, then the muttonheads muttering this leadership philosophy must be the happiest souls on earth! If you have ever uttered such nonsense, hit your knees and repent. In fact, if the casualties on whom you inflicted this drivel during the

79

course of your career are out of therapy and still willing to speak with you, apologize and beg their forgiveness.

The subject of feedback is vast. It is so instrumental in people development and accountability that I separate this challenge into two chapters. In this chapter, I address positive feedback and the consequences for failing to confront errant behaviors. In Chapter 8, I cover confrontational feedback.

THE BOOK's WISDOM AND WAY

If people do well, tell them! Proverbs 27:3 mandates, *"Do not withhold good from those to whom it is due, if it is in the power of your hand to do so."* In fact, Hebrews 3:13 reminds you to do it quickly: *". . . but exhort one another daily, while it is called 'Today,' lest any of you be hardened through the deceitfulness of sin."*

On the other hand, if someone errs or strays from the proper course, you are commissioned to address them just as quickly: *"Someone who holds back the truth causes trouble"* (Prov. 10:10).

Although you may detest an errant behavior, you must continue to love the perpetrator. In fact, confronting in love is what separates the biblically obedient from abusive bullies. There is more about this particular issue in the next chapter.

AFFIRM PUBLICLY

Most of us do not need a course in behavioral science to teach us what we have learned by personal experience throughout our lifetimes: Behaviors that are rewarded and reinforced are behaviors that are repeated. This is a simple, yet profound, concept. It is also astounding that so many leaders continue to miss the mark by failing to apply this law of human nature. Yet throughout written history, we see the value of this principle. It is not new, just largely underutilized.

After Jesus had empowered His 70 key followers to go, out two by two, into every city He was preparing to visit with instructions to heal the sick, they returned to report their success to Jesus: *"Then the seventy returned with joy, saying, 'Lord, even the demons are subject to us in Your name.' And He said to them, 'I saw Satan fall like lightning from heaven. Behold, I give you the authority to trample on serpents and scorpions, and over all the power of the enemy, and nothing shall by any means hurt you'"* (Luke 10:17–19).

Jesus rejoiced publicly over His team's success, affirming that they would do even greater things in His name. He *did not* try to keep them on their toes by bringing them down to size, or rob them of their joy with quips like, "That's what's called beginner's luck, guys. You had the easy demons, the amateurs. Don't let it go to your heads!"

As further affirmation of their success, Jesus increased their power with expanded authority. By doing so, He demonstrated that the most potent method of positive feedback goes even beyond speech and encompasses the delegation of additional discretion, empowerment, and responsibility, perfectly aligning with His promise in the Gospels that to those who use well what they have more will be given.

Jesus promised His disciples that they would go on to do even greater things than He did. This promise was validated in many ways after Christ's death. His team traveled more miles, started more churches, and preached to larger crowds than their Master during His brief tenure on earth. Christ's commitment to invest in their development, including the esteem He offered for their successes while with Him, served as a catalyst in this endeavor.

Jesus Finds and Rewards the Good in an Oppressor

I can scarcely think of a more affirming comment to ever be uttered about me than the words, "He marveled" when referring to Jesus's reaction to my faith. How about you? How long would a compliment like that keep you going? Take a look at how quickly the Master affirmed an enemy in this manner, a Roman soldier who occupied and oppressed His country:

> Now when Jesus had entered Capernaum, a centurion came to Him, pleading with Him, saying, "Lord my servant is lying at home paralyzed, dreadfully tormented." And Jesus said to him, "I will come and heal him." The centurion answered and said, "Lord, I am not worthy that You should come under my roof. But only speak a word, and my servant will be healed. For I also am a man under authority, having soldiers under me. And I say to this one, 'Go,' and he goes; and to another, 'Come,' and he comes; and to my servant, 'Do this,' and he does it." When Jesus heard it, He marveled, and said to those who followed, "Assuredly, I say to you, I have not found such great faith, not even in Israel!"
> [Matt. 8:5–10]

Throughout the Gospels, you do not read of Jesus admiring things of this world. But when He beheld the centurion's faith, he *marveled*. The Lord declared in the very presence of this man and all witnesses that this faith had not been equaled by any of the Israelites themselves. Such approbation from His mouth must have comforted the centurion nearly as much as the afflicted servant himself.

One can safely assert that nothing makes a wider breach among human beings than differences in political and religious opinions. However, the fact that this Roman instrument of suppression could earn such acclaim from Jesus bears a second look. It offers hope that in the workplace and throughout society, men and women with varied opinions and stations in life may look harder for the good in those with whom they differ and that they may rally around the positive with affirmation and assistance.

I would be remiss if I left this incident without making particular note of what exactly Christ acclaimed about the centurion. It was not the hours he worked, his title, his experience, or his particular job performance. Rather, it was the man's heart, his character, his faith, that earned the Master's praise. We are both prudent and Christ-like when we note and magnify similar characteristics in the lives of others.

FIVE RULES OF FEEDBACK

To summarize and expand on the finer points of feedback, do and remember the following:

1. Give positive feedback as quickly after an action as possible. This is because delayed consequences lessen the impact and can render feedback as little more than an afterthought.
2. Be specific rather than general. Jesus did not say, "This guy is impressive," when speaking of the centurion. Rather, he specifically pointed out exactly what was impressive: his faith. When you are specific you accomplish two things:
   - You let other people know that you care enough about them and their performance to pay attention to precisely what they did.
   - When you reinforce someone's specific behavior, that person is more likely to repeat that same behavior.

3. Patting someone on the back is not likely to make that person lazy. While there are a handful of sluggards who use reinforcement as an excuse to crawl into a hammock and take a nap, the majority will try even harder to please you in the future and to live up to the expectations they have created with solid past performance.

4. Customize feedback to the individual. You must know people to move people. Temper the style and tone of your feedback to fit the individual, without mollifying the meaning. Paul gives his young mentee, Timothy, excellent advice in this regard: *"Do not rebuke an older man, but exhort him as a father, younger men as brothers, older women as mothers, younger women as sisters, with all purity"* (1 Tim. 5:1–2).

5. Failing to confront an unsatisfactory behavior invites more of the same. This is because the absence of a consequence for a derelict act, in effect, reinforces it.

Peter Gets a Pat, Then a Punch!

Here, we will cover the pat. In the next chapter comes the punch.

You have to love the apostle Peter. He had a considerable heart, a colossal foot-sized mouth, and terrible timing! He was one of the privileged three to accompany Christ on the mountain to be transfigured, and then gushed out comments so inane during that holy moment that God simply ignored them. He was the only disciple who left the boat to walk on the water toward Jesus, only to require the Lord's rescue as his eyes left the Lord and he began sinking. Jesus trusted him as the leader of His inner circle and took James, John, and Peter to a secluded part of the Garden of Gethsemane the night He was betrayed. The result? Peter dozed off *three times* after Jesus asked him to watch and pray with Him.

On the other hand, Peter was the only disciple who fought for Jesus in the garden during His arrest, truncating an oppressor's head with his sword. Yet shortly thereafter, Peter uttered profanities and denied the very Lord he had sworn to follow to the end. After the Crucifixion, he raced to and entered Christ's empty tomb, but soon after led a boatful of other disciples, not to evangelize, but apparently to return to the fishing trade, scoring a big zero in the catch column on this particular all-nighter. Thus, it is not surprising that in the span of seven verses in Matthew, Jesus could give Peter both His most ebullient praise, and His severest rebuke! Jesus, the Master of feedback, set the standard for eliminating gray areas by letting Peter know exactly where he stood, for better and for worse.

THE APPROBATION

> When Jesus came into the region of Caesarea Philippi, He asked his disciples, saying, "Who do men say that I, the Son of Man, am?" So they said, "Some say John the Baptist, some Elijah, and others Jeremiah or one of the prophets." He said to them, "But who do you say that I am?" Simon Peter answered and said, "You are the Christ, the Son of the living God." Jesus answered and said to him, "Blessed are you, Simon Bar-Jonah, for flesh and blood has not revealed this to you, but My Father who is in heaven. And I also say to you that you are Peter, and on this rock, I will build My church, and the gates of Hades shall not prevail against it. And I will give you the keys of the kingdom of heaven, and whatever you bind on earth will be bound in heaven, and whatever you loose on earth will be loosed in heaven." [Matt. 16:16–19]

That is heavy stuff! Jesus utterly applauded Peter on the clear knowledge he possessed and affirmed that he had been taught by God, that God had shown favor to him and had set him apart for a special role that included future blessings and responsibilities.

What was spoken to Peter referred primarily, but not exclusively to him. The other apostles united with Peter in the confession; Jesus included them also in the commendation and distinction conferred upon Peter. Yet, inasmuch as Peter had demonstrated the preeminent zeal in so directly and confidently acknowledging Christ, he was honored in key respects with an exceptional reward. The Lord promised that Peter would lay the foundation of the Christian Church and be a principal force in governing it.

Jesus reinforced Peter immediately, specifically, and with clear and positive consequences established for his behavior, executing a textbook example of positive reinforcement.

Paul the Positive

Throughout his letters, the apostle Paul told it like it was. He was tough but fair, and he could certainly be blunt and confrontive, as these Scriptures demonstrate:

"Have I therefore become your enemy because I tell you the truth?"
(Gal. 4:16).
"Alexander the coppersmith did me much harm. May the Lord repay him according to his works" (2 Tim. 4:14).
"O foolish Galatians! Who has bewitched you that you should not obey the truth . . . " (Gal. 3:1).

Paul could also turn on the charm and praise. Learn from his specificity, personal commendations, uplifting language, and overall style as you read these positive excerpts from one of my favorite books of the entire Bible, Philippians:

"I thank my God upon every remembrance of you . . . " (Phil. 1:3).

"Therefore, my beloved, as you have always obeyed, not as in my presence only, but now much more in my absence, work out your own salvation with fear and trembling; for it is God who works in you both to will and to do for His good pleasure" (Phil. 2:12–13).

"But I trust in the Lord Jesus to send Timothy to you shortly, that I also may be encouraged when I know your state. For I have no one likeminded, who will sincerely care for your state. For all seek their own, not the things which are of Christ Jesus. But you know his proven character, that as a son with his father he served with me in the gospel" (Phil. 2:19–22).

"Yet I considered it necessary to send to you Epaphroditus, my brother, fellow worker, and fellow soldier . . . " (Phil. 2:25).

"But I rejoiced in the Lord greatly that now at last your care for me has flourished again . . . " (Phil. 4:10).

Some of you may be saying, "Okay, okay. So Paul could be a nice guy when he wanted to. Can't we all?" The point I wish to make goes beyond Paul's ability to remain positive and give uplifting and helpful feedback. To fully appreciate his technique, it is important to understand the conditions under which he wrote them: locked up in a foul Roman prison. In the four short chapters that comprise his letter to the Philippians, Paul used the words *joy* or *rejoice* 14 times. Perhaps this is one of the true tests of emotional maturity: Can you continue to praise and affirm others when conditions are rotten and things are not going well? It takes little effort to pat backs and issue praise when the skies are clear and the breeze is at your back. However, praising and reinforcing when you do not feel well, when you do not feel like it, when you feel down—but doing it nonetheless because it is right and effective—is a far greater test of your leadership.

87

DAVID: GREAT MONARCH, MARGINAL PAPA

Now let's move on to the consequences of failing to confront destructive behaviors or poor performance. This negligent act is a false kindness; in fact, it can be deadly.

Second Samuel, Chapter 13, tells the story of how King David's son, Amnon, raped his half-sister Tamar. Verse 21 tells us that when King David found out what happened, he became very angry. However, there is no report that he ever even discussed the crime with his offending son. "Very angry?" Are you kidding me? David's gross dereliction with no subsequent consequences is not the level of discipline you would expect Israel's greatest king to apply to his incestuous, rapist offspring. Contemplate the tragic trail of events that followed David's failure to address Amnon and hold him accountable:

1. Another of David's sons, Absalom, hated Amnon for what he did to his sister.
2. Absalom had Amnon murdered.
3. Absalom went on the run.
4. David loved Absalom too much to correct him for killing Amnon, but never forgave him completely, either, and refused to see him for years.
5. Absalom, ignored and spurned by his father, rebelled against King David, committing treason against his own father.
6. King David and his men fled Jerusalem to escape Absalom's rebellion.
7. Absalom was killed during the battle that ensued.
8. David's mourning and miseries for his dead son were so extreme that his own men accused him of being a disgrace.

David unconsciously encouraged murder and betrayal by his unwillingness to confront those he loved most. If you truly care about people, you will confront them when they err and redefine a performance expectation.

DAVID'S STRONG FINISH

To David's credit, in his 70 years on this earth, he grew wiser and more capable in parenting skills, as evidenced by his deathbed words to his son Solomon:

> Now the days of David drew near that he should die, and he charged Solomon his son, saying, "I go the way of all the earth; be strong, therefore and prove yourself a man. And keep the charge of the Lord your God: to walk in His ways, to keep His statutes, His commandments, His judgments, and His testimonies, as it is written in the Law of Moses, that you may prosper in all that you do and wherever you turn. . . ." (1 Kings 2:2–3)

David passed on feedback and instruction we can all benefit from. He stressed that knowing God's ways, statutes, commandments, judgments, and testimonies was not enough! He instructed Solomon to *keep them* and *do them*. We should resolve to do a better job of living out this advice than did Solomon, for whom it was intended. Yes, Solomon became exceedingly rich and wise. But he could not keep his hands or eyes off of foreign women: 700 wives and 300 concubines (and you thought that Samson was the Bible's strongest man). As a result, and after multiple warnings, God tore the kingdom from him.

ELI'S FOLLY

Decades before David's deficit parenting, Eli, priest of Israel, brought a curse from God on his house as a result of his failure to confront his two debauched boys. These sons are described in first

Samuel as corrupt and guilty of very great sin. Eli, the priest, did nothing about it. Read the result:

> Then the Lord said to Samuel: "Behold, I will do something in Israel at which both ears of everyone who hears it will tingle. In that day I will perform against Eli all that I have spoken concerning his house, from beginning to end. For I have told him that I will judge his house forever for the iniquity which he knows, because his sons made themselves vile, and he did not restrain them. And therefore I have sworn to the house of Eli that the iniquity of Eli's house shall not be atoned for by sacrifice or offering forever."
> [1 Sam. 3:11–14]

The five key words in this Scripture are: "... *he did not restrain them.*" I have heard leaders rationalize their failure to act and stand up to defective behaviors and performances because they believed that the problem would go away in time. But the problem does not go away; what goes away is the opportunity to correct it in its early stages!

As you can see, what you say to positively reinforce someone is just as important as what you fail to say to confront deviant behaviors or performances. The failure to confront what is wrong is a form of feedback nonetheless. In fact, it tacitly implies that the offender may continue in his or her destructive ways. When you can both reward the worthy and confront the offensive, you demonstrate the fairness and balance required to lead by THE BOOK.

Omega

"Behold, you are fair, my love! Behold, you are fair! You have dove's eyes behind your veil. Your hair is like a flock of goats, going down from Mount Gilead" (Song of Sol. 4:1).

1. Whom and what must you do a more diligent job of reinforcing positively? Which errant behaviors have you failed to confront that you must soon address?
2. To whom have you failed to provide positive feedback for a job well done? What, specifically, can you point out to that person, and how can you be more attentive to using positive reinforcement in the future?

"Well done good and faithful servant; you were faithful over a few things, I will make you ruler over many things. Enter into the joy of your lord" (Matt. 25:21).

How Do I Confront Poor Performers?

MAN'S WISDOM AND WAY

There's really no middle ground with confrontational feedback. Either you're a leadership wimp who avoids it altogether, or you step up and let people have it; and if they don't like it and leave, good riddance. You really don't need the hypersensitive types on your team, anyway. After all, you're running an organization for adults, not a day care. Besides, Galatians says that your job is to please God and not to worry about pleasing men. And what pleases God is for you to be truthful with people.

Galatians 1:10 has been hijacked by mean-spirited leaders throughout the ages who value rules over relationships and who look to justify their unloving manner of dealing with people. Here is what it says: *"For do I now persuade men or God? Or do I seek to please men? For if I still pleased men, I would not be a bondservant of Christ."*

THE BOOK's Wisdom and Way

Demonstrating love for others is what truly pleases God. Thus, we must confront, for to fail in this discipline is to evince apathy and indifference toward an individual's welfare and potential. But we must confront in love, doing so for the right reasons and with just motives. We confront to improve the character or competence of an individual, to preserve our culture, and to protect the organization's future. Confronting with feedback does not mean that you do so with the intent to punish, humiliate, expand your personal power, or edify yourself at another's expense.

When Jesus, Peter, Paul, and others confronted individuals, they customized their approach to fit the person and the offense. Their harshest words were reserved for leaders of whom more was expected and to whom more had been given. They came down harder on "heart failure" (i.e., character shortfalls) than on production issues. Despite the importance in organizations to "hit the numbers," we are wise to follow the biblical examples to take an even tougher stance against those who violate values, embrace selfishness, create division, and place their personal welfare ahead of the team's well-being. These are cancers that must be neutralized or removed, lest they devour the entire entity.

Confront with Class

Apollos is described in the book of Acts as an *"eloquent man and mighty in the Scriptures"* (Acts 18:24). This talented evangelist came to Ephesus and began preaching. Unfortunately, while his speaking style was dynamic, his knowledge of Jesus was limited. Christians named in Acts as Aquila and Priscilla heard him preaching in the synagogue and noticed his deficit of right knowledge.

What they did next demonstrated a simple, but highly effective, method for correcting and coaching someone who has strayed. Here is how Luke, author of Acts, describes this potentially contentious encounter: *"When Aquila and Priscilla heard him* [Apollos] *they took him aside and explained to him the way of God more accurately"* (Acts 18:26).

Aquila and Priscilla did not publicly rebuke Apollos. They did not embarrass him, show him up, or try to elevate their own personal standing in the synagogue by proving their superior intellect. Rather, they privately corrected and coached Apollos. This special couple subordinated their own impulses and egos to the more important task of encouraging and making more valuable a powerful worker in their cause. We are all wise to do the same, because our objective as leaders is to develop people, not punish them. Many times, team members like Apollos have great talent but lack other vital ingredients that allow them to fulfill their potential. Your responsibility is to help them maximize their talent with right knowledge, structure, and direction.

When you confront with class those in error, you will be encouraged by the words of slave-trader-turned-clergyman and author of "Amazing Grace" John Newton: "What will it profit a man if he gains his cause, and silences his adversary, if at the same time he loses that humble tender frame of spirit in which the Lord delights, and to which the promise of His presence is made."

Notice that Apollos's fault had nothing to do with a wrong heart or character arrearage. Instead, he suffered from knowledge insufficiency, which made Aquila's and Priscilla's gentle reproof even more effective and appropriate. Knowledge deficits are normally the result of ignorance, whereas heart failure is evidence of pride; the perpetrator knows better, but deliberately chooses the wrong path. Nonperformance of this nature requires vigorous opposition.

PETER AS SATAN?

While writing about positive reinforcement in the last chapter, I pointed out the Lord's effusive praise of Peter and mentioned that only a few verses later He turned on Peter and lashed out at him with His most stinging rebuke. Oh, if only Peter could have left well enough alone! But no, perhaps buoyed and puffed up by his recent acclaim, Peter opened his mouth and placed both sandals squarely in the middle of it by becoming the only disciple to castigate Christ! Read carefully and see if you can discern what was behind Peter's 12 simple words that set the Lord off: *"From that time Jesus began to show to His disciples that He must go to Jerusalem, and suffer many things from the elders and chief priests and scribes, and be killed, and be raised the third day. Then Peter took Him aside and began to rebuke Him saying, 'Far be it from You, Lord; this shall not happen to You!' But He turned and said to Peter, 'Get behind Me, Satan! You are an offense to Me, for you are not mindful of the things of God, but the things of men'"* (Matt. 16:21–23).

"Get behind Me, Satan!" Wow! Wasn't Jesus being a bit dramatic with this confrontation? I mean, this was Simon Peter, the Rock, the right-hand man of Jesus; he was not the devil. In fact, Jesus did not even speak to demons as harshly as He addressed Peter. Was it really so bad for Peter to suggest that his Lord not be killed? Absolutely! Here is why:

1. Peter was subordinating God's wisdom—he had just declared earlier that Jesus was indeed God—to his own wisdom, rebuking God in the process!
2. Peter was casting a stumbling block in his Master's way. Jesus had come from His Father to redeem humankind by his own blood. But Peter, through false compassion, would have had Him spare Himself, subordinating the salvation of a ruined world to His own comfort and ease! What could Satan himself wish for more than this?

3. Jesus also took issue with the fact that Peter magnified a carnal and worldly spirit, rather than seeking God's glory, preferring his own temporal comfort to savoring the things of God. All things considered, Peter was acting in accordance with the values and agenda of Satan, not Christ, thus earning every bit of his *"Get behind Me, Satan!"* rebuke.

4. Peter was the leader of the team. More was expected of him, and Jesus was obliged to hold him to a higher standard.

Perhaps the most important lesson to learn from this confrontation with Peter is that Jesus did not give Peter a free pass for his poor judgment just because he was in the inner circle, a top performer, the leader of the pack. Rather, He confronted him instantly and forcefully. Do not miss this point! When your own top performers are allowed to violate values, exhibit selfishness, break the rules, or otherwise minify their effort on the job without appropriate rebuke, you send a message of compromise and contradiction that countermands your culture and craters your credibility. Somehow, I doubt Jesus would have had the same reaction had Peter reported a performance failure: "Lord, I baptized only two new believers this week," or "Three members fell asleep during my sermon." It was Peter's heart failure that provoked Christ's rifle shot rebuke.

BRIDLE THE BALL-PEEN, SLING THE SLEDGE

As you read the Bible through the lens of delivering feedback, confrontation, and accountability, you will notice that the harshest words and consequences in its chapters are reserved for the violators of values issues: trespassers of godly character and integrity. There is a lesson here that you cannot afford to ignore. While performance shortfalls are significant and must be called out, a more forcible approach is required to correct matters springing from a wrong heart. In addition to Jesus's rebuke of Peter, consider Peter's own rebuke of Simon the Sorcerer and Paul's opposition to the Galatians' straying ways. You will see that to drive home their point, they put aside the ball-peen hammer and reached for the sledge.

Acts 8 tells the story of Peter's encounter with Simon the Sorcerer. Simon had become wealthy by performing black magic, but had apparently changed his ways and had been baptized by Philip. When John and Peter came to town and began praying for the new believers to be filled with the Holy Spirit, here is what happened:

> And when Simon saw that through the laying on of the apostle's hands the Holy Spirit was given, he offered them money, saying, "Give me this power also, that anyone on whom I lay hands may receive the Holy Spirit." But Peter said to him, "Your money perish with you, because you thought that the gift of God could be purchased with money! You have neither part nor portion in this matter, for your heart is not right in the sight of God. Repent therefore of this your wickedness, and pray God if perhaps the thoughts of your heart may be forgiven you. For I see that you are poisoned by bitterness and bound by iniquity." [Acts 8:18–23]

Perhaps mindful of having been rebuked by Jesus years earlier for his own wrong heart, Peter assailed Simon the Sorcerer's corrupt heart. It mattered not that Simon had money or that he was a newer member of the team. Peter knew that "heart issues" must be addressed with vigor.

The apostle Paul was no politically correct pulpit pundit, either. His letter to the Galatians confronted those who had drifted from

98

the vision and teaching he had laid out for them. Their hearts had left the truth and chased false teachings and teachers.

Galatians was the first letter included in the Bible that Paul wrote, and he hit the ground running: *"I marvel that you are turning away so soon from Him who called you in the grace of Christ; to a different gospel, which is not another; but there are some who trouble you and want to pervert the gospel of Christ. But even if we, or an angel from heaven, preach any other gospel to you than what we have preached to you, let him be accursed"* (Gal. 1:6–9).

In Paul's letter to his troubleshooter, Titus, he gives clear instructions for how Titus is to accost false teachers in the churches of Crete: *"For there are many insubordinate, both idle talkers and deceivers, especially those of the circumcision* [the Jews], *whose mouths must be stopped, who subvert whole households, teaching things which they ought not, for the sake of dishonest gain. One of them, a prophet of their own said, 'Cretans are always liars, evil beasts, lazy, gluttons.' This testimony is true. Therefore rebuke them sharply; that they may be sound in the faith, not giving heed to Jewish fables and commandments of men who turn from the truth"* (Titus 1:10–14).

Note again that, in both cases, Paul was primarily focusing his assault on character deficits: lack of faith, their wandering hearts, and their misplaced affections.

A FALSE KINDNESS

Some leaders feel it is harsh to rebuke others, so they choose instead to ignore errant behaviors. While these same leaders may excel at patting the back, they fall short in caring enough to confront followers who stray. This lack of feedback and consequences following poor performance encourages more of the same. Effective leaders learn to "shovel the piles while they are small." They face problem issues early on with firmness and fairness, before the behaviors have a chance to infect the culture or evolve into bad habits that are nearly impossible to change. You may recall the consequences that Eli and David suffered for their failure to confront their offspring, mentioned in Chapter 7.

You cannot afford to become overly concerned about how people receive your feedback. You cannot control, nor are you responsible for, their responses. Your duty is to tell the truth in love. Hopefully, the receivers of your words will have read Proverbs 15:32. If not, you may find it helpful to refer them to it: *"He who disdains instruction despises his own soul. But he who heeds rebuke gets understanding."*

CHOOSE YOUR BATTLES

Samuel Johnson once said, "The art of being wise is in knowing what to overlook." In other words, choose your battles carefully. Here are some biblical tips to help shape your perspective in this regard:

- *"Do not strive with a man without cause; if he has done you no harm"* (Prov. 3:30).
- *"Do not answer a fool according to his folly, lest you also be like him"* (Prov. 26:4).
- *"When He came in, He said to them, 'Why make this commotion and weep? The child is not dead, but sleeping.' And they ridiculed Him. But when He had put them all outside, He took the father and the mother of the child, and those who were with Him, and entered where the child was lying"* (Mark 5:39–40).
- *"Then Pilate said to Him, 'Do You not hear how many things they testify against You?' But He answered him not one word, so that the governor marveled greatly"* (Matt. 27:13–14).

100

If a top performer in my company who is never late for work rushes in tardy one day, I am not going to lecture that person about our "attention-to-detail" or "urgency" core values or shout out sarcastically, "Good afternoon!" Instead, I will ask with genuine concern, "Is everything all right with you today?" On the other hand, if an employee who has already established a suspect track record with us shows up late, I will handle it differently. (I cover this particular instance in greater detail in Chapter 9.)

Does this mean that I am compromising our core values for employees who are top performers? Absolutely not. I am simply giving someone who has established a credible track record of integrity with our organization the benefit of the doubt for a minor, first-time offense. Had this same person committed a more egregious error, such as lying to a customer, I would handle it far more forcefully.

FOLLOW UP FEEDBACK WITH FOLLOW-THROUGH

You can maximize the effects of feedback when you follow through to warn, offer further instruction, or encourage the subject of your critique. In John 5:8–9, at the Pool of Bethesda, Jesus healed a man who had been lame for 38 years with these simple words: *"Rise, take up your bed and walk."*

Since it was the Sabbath, the religious officials told the cured man that it was unlawful for him to carry the bed he had lain on for nearly four full decades! Can you imagine the nerve these so-called men of God, chastising him for carrying a symbol of his former infirmity—the same man they themselves had been unable to heal despite their high religious status?

Jesus then found this man in the temple for a bit of follow-through: *"See, you have been made well. Sin no more, lest a worse thing come upon you"* (John 5:14).

Following through in a like manner after offering feedback gives you an opportunity to reaffirm, further direct, or bring closure to your prior instruction.

Do Not Rehash the Past

When confronting another, it is common to unload both barrels upon the victim by rehearsing all past sins in order to create a crescendo for the presentation of new and current offenses. Do not do this! It creates bitterness and breaks trust.

In John 21, after Jesus had appeared to the disciples on the seashore following the Resurrection, He endeavored to restore Peter. This was after Peter's miserable failure, denying Christ three times on the night of his arrest. To help Peter atone for the three denials, the Lord asked him three questions that would afford Peter the opportunity to reaffirm his love for Jesus, three being the identical number of times Peter had earlier disowned Him:

> So when they had eaten breakfast, Jesus said to Simon Peter, "Simon, son of Jonah, do you love Me more than these?" He said to Him, "Yes, Lord: You know that I love You." He said to him, "Feed my lambs." He said to him again a second time, "Simon, son of Jonah, do you love Me?" He said to Him, "Yes, Lord: You know that I love You." He said to him, "Tend my sheep." He said to him the third time, "Simon, son of Jonah, do you love Me?" Peter was grieved because He said to him

the third time, "Do you love Me?" And he said to Him, "Lord, You know all things; You know that I love You." Jesus said to him, "Feed My sheep." [John 21:15–17]

There are three primary points to note in this exchange:

1. Jesus asked Peter, *"Do you love me more than these?"* yet no one is sure to what Jesus referred to as *"these."* It may have been the fish that Peter had just caught—153 large ones—as Peter seemed inclined to abandon evangelism and return to his former trade.
2. *"Feed my lambs," "Feed my sheep,"* and *"Tend my sheep"* were feedback phrases from Jesus that referred to Peter's mission to teach and lead both new (lambs) and mature (sheep) followers of Christ.
3. At no time during this follow-through did Jesus remind Peter of his three denials—the most significant failures of his life. Nor did He go back further and rehearse Peter's impulsiveness in slicing off the servant's ear with a sword in the Garden of Gethsemane during His arrest. Rather, Jesus focused on building him up and defining fresh expectations for the future.

When confronting a character or performance shortfall, your purpose should not be to build up a case against the person by piling on with condemnation and judgment. Rather, your sole objective is to help both the person and his or her performance improve. Period.

OMEGA

"So the Lord became angry with Solomon, because his heart had turned from the Lord God of Israel, who had appeared to him twice, and had commanded him concerning this thing, that he should not go after other gods; but he did not keep what the Lord had commanded" (1 Kings 11:9–10).

1. Are you courageous enough to confront your top people for "heart failure" issues?
2. Are there instances when you have turned a blind eye to heart failure as long as an individual was "hitting the numbers"?

"Reject a divisive man after the first and second admonition, knowing that such a person is warped and sinning, being self-condemned" (Titus 3:10).

What Are Core Values, and How Do They Benefit My Organization?

MAN'S WISDOM AND WAY

Core values are little more than a load of Pollyannaish-happy-hot-tub talk. Consultants promote their creation so that you'll hire them to help you come up with them. In challenging times, we need to stay focused, and the last thing we need is another exercise in academic nonsense. Business schools dream up this core value stuff to make our lives more complicated. In the real world, we need production, not slogans. We can't afford to become distracted from our pursuit of hard numbers by a bunch of touchy-feely prattle like core values. Creating core values ranks right up there with trivial pursuits like conjuring up mission and vision statements. While we're at it, let's huddle up each morning in the lobby to join hands and sing "Kumbaya."

The preceding paragraph is a near-verbatim statement I personally made in my first management job. This was long ago, when I was under the illusion that my new title confirmed that I was a leader and that my promotion had miraculously made me smarter. I know that I am not yet nearly what I should be, but I thank God that I am not what I used to be.

THE BOOK's WISDOM AND WAY

The Bible abounds with instances of God creating and communicating the nonnegotiable behaviors that He expected His people to live by. The Ten Commandments and Christ's Sermon on the Mount are prime examples. Essential leadership responsibilities are creating, living, and holding others accountable for core values. Core values serve multiple purposes:

1. Core values create the DNA of your organization. They differentiate you from competitors.
2. Core values make it easier for employees to know what to do in situations where they cannot check with authorities or ask for permission.
3. Core values provide a filter to help you hire the right people.
4. Core values provide a filter to help you fire the wrong people.
5. Core values help create a culture that supports your vision.
6. Core values provide a benchmark for behavioral accountability.

Years ago, team members who violated values and possessed a dearth of character were pariahs. In a sad indictment of our times, the opposite often proves to be true. Contemporary outcasts are those souls who refuse to cede their principles, those who forgo what is easy or popular for what is right. In some circles, these principled Daniels and Ruths are rewarded with mockery, ostracizing, and vindictiveness. By failing to create and enforce core values that champion these heroes and weed out offenders, you aid the offenders and cheat your champions.

SAMPLE VALUES FROM THE MASTER

When Jesus began His ministry, one of His first orders of business was to communicate the core values of what would become the Christian faith. For a short course of what core values look like, read Matthew 5–7. Here are seven samples of what were destined to become, and remain, the core values—the behavioral compass—of a Christian.

1. **Be a light!**
   "Let your light so shine before men, that they may see your good works and glorify your Father in heaven" (Matt. 5:16).

2. **Reconcile quickly!**
   "Therefore if you bring your gift to the altar, and there remember that your brother has something against you, leave your gift there before the altar, and go your way. First be reconciled to your brother, and then come and offer your gift" (Matt. 5:23–24).

3. **Give straight answers!**
   "But let your 'Yes' be 'Yes,' and your 'No,' 'No.' For whatever is more than these is from the evil one" (Matt. 5:37).

4. **Go the second mile!**
   "And whoever compels you to go one mile, go with him two" (Matt. 5:41).

5. Love your enemies!

"But I say to you, love your enemies, bless those who curse you, do good to those who hate you, and pray for those who spitefully use you and persecute you" (Matt. 5:44).

6. Do not worry!

"Therefore I say to you, do not worry about your life, what you will eat or what you will drink; not about your body what you will put on. Is not life more than food and the body more than clothing?" (Matt. 6:25).

7. Put God first!

"But seek first the Kingdom of God and His righteousness, and all these things shall be added to you" (Matt. 6:33).

Christ's values were, and are, clear. It is very likely that His listeners did not say, "Hmmm, I wonder what He means by that." And this is true of Christianity today. It is not that people do not know what Jesus or the Bible says about how they are to live. They know full well, but do not like it or try to find a way around it!

OUR FIVE CORPORATE CORE VALUES

I will share the values of our company, Dave Anderson's LearnToLead, not because they should be your own values or because they are perfect. I share them because I can speak credibly about how powerful they have been in creating our high-performance culture, in influencing team member behaviors, and as a filter for hiring and firing.

At our company, we do more than simply list the value. We also include a sentence that demonstrates what the value looks like in practice. This helps us to more specifically reinforce healthy behaviors and confront toxic behaviors as they manifest. If you simply declare a value but fail to define it, some employees may interpret the value in a manner that best suits their agenda or comfort zone. For instance, a selfish associate is prone to twist a value of "Teamwork" to mean: "Since I am the top performer here, the *team works* for me!

Here are our five core values:

1. *Teamwork*. Teamwork means that the good of the team comes before the personal comfort or agenda of any individual team member.

2. *Integrity*. Integrity means that we always do what is right, not what is easy, cheap, popular or convenient—and we do so without excuse and regardless of the cost.

3. *Urgency*. Urgency means that we serve one another and customers quickly and find reasons to do things *now* rather than to delay, debate, or procrastinate.

4. *Personal growth*. Personal growth means that we are all expected to work as hard on improving ourselves as on getting better at our jobs. Personal improvement is not an option.

5. *Attention to detail*. Attention to detail means that we will become brilliant in the basics and pay attention to getting things done right the first time! We will become faithful in the little things.

LESS IS MORE

It is not feasible to create core values to espouse each behavior you deem important within your organization. A client once boasted to me that his organization had 14 core values. "Wonderful!" I exclaimed. "There were only Ten Commandments, but I'm sure your 14 values are excellent. Incidentally, can you please list them all for me?" He could not. As coach Vince Lombardi used to say, "It's hard to be aggressive when you're confused."

Some of your values will overlap and cover additional important behaviors without having to itemize those specific behaviors. For instance, the folks in our company know that they must be at work on time. We do not need a value for this because several of our other values address this: integrity, teamwork, urgency, and attention to detail.

During His Sermon on the Mount, Jesus did not say anything specifically against incest, bestiality, orgies, homosexuality, or fornication. However, He did say this: *"You have heard that it was said to those of old, 'You shall not commit adultery.' But I say to you that whoever looks at a woman to lust for her has already committed adultery with her in his heart"* (Matt. 5:27–28).

Everyone fully understood that by raising the standard for sexual purity from the Old Testament commandment of "Do not commit adultery" to the new benchmark that said, "Don't even *look* upon another with lust," Jesus did not approve of any form of sexual immorality. He was not expected to itemize dozens of explicit expectations to cover each possible sexual offense. His clearly stated value condemning something as supposedly harmless as just looking upon another person with lust made clear His expectations in regard to sexual morality across the board.

A Blueprint for Decision Making

If your core values do not influence the daily behaviors of your people, they are impotent. One of the many benefits of values is that they make it easier for employees to make decisions and to know how to handle certain situations. Our company's five core values are posted prominently in our conference room, where I often point to them during employee reviews and team meetings. My wife, Rhonda, runs our business while I spend the majority of my time speaking, writing, and creating new material. She often travels with me to various engagements, which means our team must be able to make decisions, seize opportunities, and solve problems without being able to immediately seek our approval.

One December, a client called in to place an $800 order for various DVDs. The team member taking the order knew that the following week we were going to send an e-mail blast advertising a year-end sale to clear out inventory, which would reduce the client's cost by half. Because this employee fully understood that our value of integrity means to always do the right thing, he was able to make a decision to give the discount to the customer and reduce the purchase price by $400—without having to check with a supervisor. The customer was blown away by the service he received from a frontline employee. Rhonda and I further validated our employee's integrity by publicly pointing out to all team members the rightness of his decision and that it was exactly what we expected.

Failing to support those who live your values renders your values farcical. And failing to live your values as a leader labels your leadership laughable. Just as, over the centuries, Christians who confessed Christ with their mouths but denied Him with their lifestyles gave rise to atheism, your failure to walk your talk stimulates bitterness, resentment, and broken trust within your organization.

A Blueprint for Hiring

If you use your core values as a blueprint for hiring, you will not make the mistake of diminishing your hiring principles to solve staffing shortages or of hiring talented people without the right character traits. Jesus raised the bar for human behavior and expected others to strive to "enter [His kingdom] through the narrow gate." You must also create a narrow gate whereby people must earn the right to work in your organization.

Jesus never lowered His expectations to accommodate the moral emptiness of another. This is news to some misguided Christians who want to believe that Christ, with all of His grace and mercy, came to judge them more leniently than the laws of the Old Testament. Or they convince themselves that their loving Papa-in-the-Sky will institute no judgment at all. These beliefs find their root in hell itself and demonstrate a glaring ignorance of Christ's own words. Understanding the importance of following Jesus's example of setting and sticking to high standards is an essential part of inculcating your core values into your culture. Take heart and learn from how your Master raised the bar:

- As presented in this chapter, Christ raised the standard in defining adultery. He did not drop it to delight the debauched.
- You may also recall the instance where He raised the bar in Matthew 5:43: *"You have heard that it was said, 'You shall love your neighbor and hate your enemy.' But I say to you, love your enemies, bless those who curse you, do good to those who hate you, and pray for those who spitefully use you and persecute you."*
- Taking the classic commandment from Leviticus 19:18, *"You shall not take vengeance, nor bear any grudge against the children of your people, but you shall love your neighbor as yourself,"* Jesus redefined a sky-high standard in John 13:34 with this: *"A new commandment I give to you, that you love one another; as I have loved you, that you also love one another."* He elevated the expectation that we should love our neighbors as ourselves to one of loving as Christ loves—in other words, unconditionally!

When you create and enforce core values, hold your ground! John 6:60 tells us: *"Therefore many of His disciples, when they heard this, said, 'This is a hard saying; who can understand it.'"* But Jesus did not lower the bar to make it easier for them to perceive, conceive, or understand. Just a few verses later, here is what transpired: *"From that time many of His disciples went back and walked with Him no more"* (John 6:66). There is no report of Jesus, just to keep onboard those who wished to walk away, chasing after them, begging, pleading, or compromising what He had declared to be important. He let them go. And so should you. However, the best time to lose them over values issues is before you hire them!

Carefully present the values and gauge your applicants' responses. Listen to what they say and also to what they do not say. Do they ask questions, flinch a bit, or ask for clarification? When you have precise criteria against which to measure a job applicant, it eases decision making. Just as sheep standing before a green background appear white, those same sheep standing before a white background become a dirty gray. Your values serve as the white background, enabling you to more easily detect the dirty gray in your job applicants.

A BLUEPRINT TO FIRE

"Allan" was a competent performer for our company, but we fired him anyway. Why? His competence did not compensate for his compulsion to violate our values.

Allan's problem was that he could not manage to make it to work on time. A little thing, you say? No way. It violated four of our values: teamwork, attention to detail, urgency, and integrity.

The fact that we had preestablished values made it easier to do two things:

1. Confront Allan with his errant behavior, as we could point out that he had violated our values and give him a chance to correct it.
2. Increase the speed and ease with which we terminated Allan when his unacceptable behavior continued.

You may also rest assured that after Allan's dismissal, everyone in our organization was reassured that our values are more than decor on the wall, more than an academic exercise. To that end, here is a quick checklist to help you assess and improve the status of your own core values:

❑ Do you have them? Do your people know them? More important, do they live them?
❑ Do the leaders live the values?
❑ Are the values visible?
❑ Are the values affirmed in public when displayed by team members?
❑ Are team members who violate the values quickly confronted and reschooled on your expectations?
❑ Do you measure prospective employees against your values before hiring them?
❑ Do you measure team members against the values during reviews?
❑ Do your values influence the daily behaviors of your team members?
❑ If a random selection of five team members were asked to write down the values, as well as a descriptive sentence of what they look like in practice, would all of their answers be identical?
❑ When was the last time you publicly spoke about your values to team members?

ONE BAD ACHAN CAN SPOIL THE WHOLE BUNCH

Achan is a somewhat obscure Bible character, but his anonymity cannot hide the fact that his one sin caused his entire people to suffer. Contemporary leaders can learn an important lesson from his actions concerning the importance of having *everyone* in an organization embrace and live by established core values.

The Israelites were preparing to attack Jericho and begin their conquest of the Promised Land. God was with them and their victories were assured. Joshua, their leader gave instructions: *"Shout, for the Lord has given you the city! Now the city shall be doomed by the Lord to destruction, it and all who are in it. Only Rahab the harlot shall live, she and all who are with her in the house, because she hid the messengers that we sent. And you, by all means abstain from the accursed things, lest you become accursed when you take of the accursed things, and make the camp of Israel a curse and trouble it"* (Joshua 6:16–19).

After the Israelis easily conquered Jericho, something went wrong. They lost the very next battle, a no-brainer against tiny and weak Ai. In fact, the Israeli spies doing reconnaissance work in Ai were so confident of victory that they recommended sending only 2,000 to 3,000 people into battle. But the men of Ai quickly killed 36 Israelis, chased them, and struck them down as they retreated.

Joshua was in shock, fell to his face, and cried out before the Lord. His unbecoming words to God demonstrated a lack of trust reminiscent of the rebellious spirit the masses demonstrated as they complained against God in the wilderness.

God would have none of Joshua's whining:

> So the Lord said to Joshua, "Get up! Why do you lie thus on your face? Israel has sinned and they have also transgressed My covenant which I commanded them. For they have even taken some

115

of the accursed things, and have both stolen and deceived; and they have also put it among their own stuff. Therefore the children of Israel could not stand before their enemies, but turned their backs before their enemies because they have become doomed to destruction. Neither will I be with you anymore, unless you destroy the accursed from among you. Get up, sanctify the people, and say, 'Sanctify yourselves for tomorrow, because thus says the Lord God of Israel: There is an accursed thing in your midst, O Israel; you cannot stand before your enemies until you take away the accursed thing from among you.'" [Josh. 7:10–13]

To make a long story short, in defiance of the values established by the Lord and reinforced by Joshua, Achan had looted the enemy and hid the haul in his tent. Under pressure, Achan admitted his transgression and was stoned, the accursed items he swiped were burned, and Israel regained God's favor.

Eight Useful Takeaways from This Story

1. It does not take six "bad ones" to corrupt your culture. All it takes is one!
2. When one team member abuses the values, the entire team suffers.
3. The team and culture cannot be fully restored to health until the perpetrator is held accountable for his or her behavior.
4. Cancers like Achan will infect and affect others unless their behaviors are changed or they are removed.
5. Violators of values must be dealt with immediately.

116

6. Achan was not given multiple chances to get his act together before he was held accountable.

7. Do you have an Achan on your team? Here is a more important question: Why?

8. Do not doubt for a moment that God hates sin so deeply that He is willing to punish many for the sins of one. He does, He has, and He will continue to do so.

How Do Core Values Differ from Vision and Mission?

There is often confusion over the differences between vision, mission, and core values. Perhaps this will simplify it.

1. *Vision* is direction. It should be specific and measurable.

Jesus cast the vision for His church in Matthew 28:19: *"Go therefore and make disciples of all nations, baptizing them in the name of the Father and of the Son and of the Holy Spirit, teaching them to observe all the things I have commanded you . . ."*

Jesus's vision is measurable: *"all nations,"* and *"all the things I have commanded you."* This vision unites His followers today and gives them a common goal to rally around and work toward.

Do you have a specific vision that unites your entire team? While you may have a long-term vision for what you expect to accomplish in a decade, it is best to roll the minivision objectives in smaller increments of time. Long-term visions without shorter-term goals take the pressure of doing enough in the present to make a dent in the status quo. Incidentally, if you know the vision but your team does not, you must work immediately to bring the vision from "me" to "we," because you can't achieve an organizational vision solo.

2. *Mission* is purpose. Mission is more general than vision.

Living your mission will help lead to the fulfillment of your vision. An organizational mission statement is really a purpose statement. Do not confuse this with the quantifiable vision with specific metrics. Jesus declared His mission/purpose in Mark 10:45: *"For even the Son of Man did not come to be served, but to serve, and to give His life a ransom for many."* In this one powerful sentence Jesus declared the most potent mission statement in history.

By living His mission, Jesus gained an audience and broadened His platform, and He served as an example for His followers to emulate so that they could do the same and achieve His vision in the process. In fact, Romans 8:29 mandates that we make the mission of Jesus our own: *"For whom He foreknew, He also predestined to be conformed to the image of His Son."*

As we conform our character and life to Christ's, we embrace His mission and are able to progress toward the ultimate vision of making disciples of all nations and teaching them all that Jesus has taught us. Likewise, living the mission statement created for your organization enables you to advance toward your own vision.

3. Finally, *core values* help create the culture necessary to support the mission and facilitate attainment of the vision.

Aligning and channeling these three elements of clarity provides a combustible force to transform and elevate your culture. Chapter 12 in this book will more specifically explain the role of a healthy culture in your organization—and how to create that culture so that it supports your vision.

You cannot expect to be able to lead by THE BOOK until you create, bring to life, hold others accountable for, and personally live a handful of nonnegotiable core values that become your organization's DNA. Core values tell the world that you've decided to stand for something and that you're less likely to fall for the wrong things.

OMEGA

"Then the Lord God took the man and put him in the Garden of Eden to tend and keep it. And the Lord God commanded the man, saying, 'Of every tree of the garden you may freely eat; but of the tree of knowledge of good and evil you shall not eat, for in the day that you eat of it you shall surely die'" (Gen. 2:15–17).

1. What are your core values? Must you create, expand, narrow, or redefine them?
2. How many values violators are currently on your team? What will you do to either turn them around or remove them?

"Now I urge you brethren, note those who cause divisions and offenses, contrary to the doctrine which you learned; and avoid them" (Rom. 16:17).

How Do I Balance My Work and Home Life?

MAN'S WISDOM AND WAY

My family understands that the long hours I spend at work is the sacrifice we all make to live a comfortable life. Besides, we've learned that the quality of time we spend together is more important than the quantity of time. While it may be tough for them to fully understand the career investment I'm making now, some day they will appreciate what I'm doing for them.

Many leaders earn well but they do not live well. They sacrifice their family, health, friends, and relationship with God for more stuff, promotions, and power. They work hard to secure a golden retirement and add years to their life. In the process, they fail to add life to their years. This is foolishness, because those who add years to their life without adding life to their years merely perpetuate the depth and duration of their emptiness.

THE BOOK's Wisdom and Way

Any Christian feigning confusion over what should be most important in his or her life should win an Academy Award for best actor. The Bible makes resolutely clear in Matthew 6:33 the proper ordering of one's priorities. You can rest assured that balance, provision, and happiness in *all* other sectors of your life are contingent upon getting this right: *"But seek first the Kingdom of God and His righteousness, and all these things shall be added to you"* (Matt. 6:33). I assume that since Jesus did not waffle, stutter, or hesitate in making this statement, you caught the intended sequence for your life's priorities.

In the book of John, Jesus reveals the secret for bearing much fruit in your life. Again, there are no gray areas: *"I am the vine, you are the branches. He who abides in Me, and I in him, bears much fruit; for without Me you can do nothing"* (John 15:5).

Frankly, if your relationship with God is not what it should be, your relationship with others, including those living under your roof, who should mean the most to you, will suffer and fail to reach its potential.

What your family needs more than your paycheck, a big house, nice cars, a college education, or fancy vacations is spiritual leadership from a mom and dad who have made their relationship with God *the* priority in their lives. Only after your heart is humble enough to rank God first in your life will you ever be able to properly value your family.

This means that the question, "How do I balance my family and work life?" is actually the wrong question. The right question is, "What must I *first* do to prioritize family and work?" The answer is that only as you subordinate both family and work to God will you ever be able to prioritize family and work.

122

LEARN FROM THE GREEDY RULER

The underlying principle in this chapter's "THE BOOK's Wisdom and Way" is so vital to successful work-life balance that we need to return for a moment to Chapter 6, where I related how the rich young ruler flinched and failed in the face of his tough interview with Jesus. As you revisit the famous encounter, evaluate the root of this fellow's misguided priorities, especially since it can help you avoid the same error.

When addressed by Jesus, the young man showed that, unlike many in his day, he had consistently tried to do what is right in every human relationship, affirming that he had indeed followed the commandments Jesus listed.

But each of the commands quoted by Jesus when instructing the fellow what he was to do in Mark 10:19 came from the "second tablet" of the Ten Commandments. That tablet sets standards for human-to-human relationships. Even more important was how the ruler dealt with the commandments from the "first tablet," commands that deal with an individual's personal relationship with the Lord. This is because how you deal with God directly influences how you deal with human beings. Jesus decided to test the ruler's devotion to the standard of the first tablet with these words: *"Go sell your possessions and give to the poor. . . . Then come, follow Me"* (Mark 10:21). His invitation was designed to show the young man that his possessions came before God. The text tells us that the individual "went away sad," for he was wealthy. In a choice between God, in the person of the Son of God, and money, this young man chose money. Because his relationship with God was not what it should have been, the ruler unwittingly confessed that his relationships with people were not up to par, either—thus contradicting his earlier assertion that he always followed those particular commandments.

The first of the Ten Commandments is, *"You shall have no other gods before Me"* (Exod. 20:3). No matter how craftily you may rationalize the health of your relationships with others, including your own family, unless you love God supremely, you will certainly fail to fulfill the potential for love, joy, and growth within your family.

THE KEY TO LOVING GOD

Despite what you might think, the key to loving God is not in knowing the Bible. In fact, just reading the Bible will not make you a better Christian any more than reading the *Wall Street Journal* will make you a better businessperson. You must act upon what you know! For example, the devil knows the Bible, and he quoted Scripture to Jesus in the Wilderness, but he does not love God or His ways. The first step to loving God is obeying what He says in His Word. In Jesus's own words, here is the key to loving Him: *"If you love Me, keep My commandments"* (John 14:15). And then again: *"He who has My commandments and keeps them, it is he who loves Me. And he who loves Me will be loved by My Father, and I will love him and manifest Myself to him"* (John 14:21). And yet again: *"Jesus answered and said to him, 'If anyone loves Me, he will keep My word; and My Father will love him and We will come to him and make Our home with him'"* (John 14:23).

Notice what is and is not blessed by Jesus in the following Scripture: *"If you know these things blessed are you if you do them"* (John 13:17). Did you catch it? *Knowing* is not acclaimed; it is not enough; *doing* is! Here is the same message again: *"Therefore whoever hears these sayings of Mine, and does them, I will liken to a wise man who built his house on the rock . . ."* (Matt. 7:24).

The blessings of a properly ordered life begin to manifest as you faithfully place God before all other gods (money, job, hobbies, etc.) in your life. In recognition of your obedience, the Spirit then leads and enables you to prioritize your family and job in a manner that brings maximum fulfillment and success in both arenas. If you have been pursuing family-work balance, but have skipped this important first step, you are off track and need to make a course correction.

To Know Him Is to Obey Him

Since *doing* is essential, rest assured that the more you know about God, His love, and His ways, the more you will *want* to obey Him. Obeying God is not a chore or a sentence to serve for those who love Him. Rather, it is a joy and a privilege. There can be no greater objective for the serious and committed Christian than to make a lifelong quest of coming to know Christ and obeying His Word. Not just believe in Him or know about Him, but really *know* Him, follow Him, and conform to His commands.

In Philippians 3:8–9, the apostle Paul claimed that everything he had ever owned, currently possessed, or would possess in the future was utter rubbish compared to knowing Christ. *"Yet indeed I also count all things loss for the excellence of the knowledge of Christ Jesus my Lord, for whom I have suffered the loss of all things, and count them as rubbish, that I may gain Christ and be found in Him . . ."* (Phil. 3:8–9).

When King David was dying and giving final instructions to his son and successor, Solomon, he did not say:

"Be a good king."
"Live a good life."
"Believe in God."

Rather, he admonished his son to know and *obey* God, realizing that the more his son knew God, the more likely he would be to obey Him.

> Now the days of David drew near that he should die, and he charged Solomon his son, saying: 'I go the way of all the earth; be strong, therefore, and prove yourself a man. And keep the charge of the Lord our God; to walk in His ways, to keep His statutes, His commandments, His judgment, and His testimonies, as it is written in the Law of Moses, that you may prosper in all that you do and wherever you turn. . . .' [1 Kings 2:2–3]

In the Bible, God repeatedly tells us that if we seek Him, we will find Him. We will be able to build a relationship with Him. We will know His mind, will, and desires. God does this because He loves people. He knows that we will love people like we should only when we love Him like we should. This is why Matthew 22:37–39 is worded as it is. Notice the order. You must first love God completely before you can love others as God directs — including your own family members: *"Jesus said to him, 'You shall love the Lord your God with all your heart, with all your soul, and with all your mind. This is the first and great commandment. And the second is like it: You shall love your neighbor as yourself.'"*

THE CYCLE OF VIRTUE

All this talk of the blessings that come with knowing God and doing what He says provokes the question, do you *know* Him? How hard are you even trying? Here is a hint: You cannot possibly know Him if you spend little or no time with Him! The fact is that however close you are to Christ at this very moment is the result of your own decisions. You are as close as you choose to be. Sadly, if you have chosen not to know Him well, you are less likely to obey Him, and living in disobedience wreaks havoc on both your work and home life. Think of attaining work-life balance as a sequence you follow, as set forth in the six points in this cycle of virtue:

1. Seek first and foremost to know God.
2. The more you know about God, His love, and His ways, the more you will love Him.
3. The more you love God, the more you will obey Him.
4. As you obey Him, you will continue to put Him first and love Him with all of your heart, soul, and mind, as commanded by Scripture.
5. While you are in a proper relationship with God, your right heart will enhance your relationships with others, adding a joyful and healthy life balance to your home life.
6. These enhanced relationships at home will evoke a greater sense of personal fulfillment that you will bring with you back into the workplace, making you even more effective than before.

These six steps create a cycle of virtue that takes you far beyond the worn out "You-have-to-make-time-for-quality-time" palaver dispensed on TV by the latest "Dr. So-and-So," talk show hosts, and celebrities—many of whom seem to believe that their vast experiences in sinful relationships and multiple divorces qualifies them as relationship gurus.

In his letter to the Ephesians, Paul offers outstanding relationship advice to husbands, wives, children, and parents that can take place only if one is on the cycle of virtue. You have to reach item 5 on the cycle of virtue for Paul's instructions to fully benefit your life. Notice how the following biblical instructions and principles tie together, yet all are based on putting God first:

1. *"Husbands love your wives, just as Christ also loved the church and gave Himself for her . . ."* (Eph. 5:23).

   How did Christ love the church? He loved it completely, put its interests before His own comfort or agenda, served it, protected it, provided all He had for its benefit, and gave His life for it. No human is likely to so love another person so completely—regardless of who that person is—unless and until he or she has first loved God completely and surrendered to being led by the Holy Spirit.

2. *"Nevertheless, let each one of you in particular so love his own wife as himself, and let the wife see that she respects her husband"* (Eph. 5:33).

   In case loving one's wife as Christ also loved the church did not get husbands' attention, Paul made it more personal and instructed us to love our wives as we love ourselves. He then instructed wives to respect their husbands. But the order in which the instructions are listed is important. This is because a woman is not likely to respect a man who does not treat her lovingly. And the man is not likely to treat his spouse as lovingly as he should unless his heart is humble enough to place God first in his life and love Him completely. This reinforces the entire thrust of this chapter that true fulfillment at work cannot be achieved until there is a loving harmony in the home; this, in turn, is not going to happen until each partner has a pure and loving heart that can come only from an intimate relationship with God.

3. *"Children, obey your parents in the Lord. . . . And you, fathers, do not provoke your children to wrath, but bring them up in the training and admonition of the Lord"* (Eph. 6:1–4).

By now, I am sure you see the pattern: Children are far more likely to honor and obey parents if their parents treat them lovingly and raise them in the Lord's ways— teaching the children to put God first in their own lives, just as the parents have done. However, parents who do not have the heart to put God first are also not likely to treat their children well, provoking them, overcontrolling them, and creating bitterness and resentment. This in turn causes the children to despise and rebel against their parents.

The apostle John offered some of the most helpful advice for learning to love God and put Him first in our lives by following Christ's own example: *"But whoever keeps His word, truly the love of God is perfected in him. By this we know that we are in Him. He who says he abides in Him ought himself also to walk just as He walked"* (1 John 2:5).

MARY HAD THE "ONE THING"

In Luke 10:38–41, Jesus was at the house of his friends Martha and Mary, who lived in Bethany, just outside of Jerusalem. Martha was busy with much preparing and serving, while Mary sat at the feet of Jesus and listened to His words so that she might know Him better. Here is what happened next when a perturbed Martha approached Jesus: *"Lord, do You not care that my sister has left me to serve alone? Therefore tell her to help me. And Jesus answered and said to her, 'Martha, Martha, you are worried and troubled about many things. But one thing is needed, and Mary has chosen that good part, which will not be taken away from her'"* (Luke 10:38–41).

In case you missed the "one thing" needed that so engrossed Mary, I refer you to the first of the six steps in the cycle of virtue I offered earlier.

What business do you need to put aside so that you may come to more fully know Him? For some of you, it is mindless radio and television. For others, it is an obsession with your hobbies, Web surfing, Twitter, or a party lifestyle. If you spend more time reading *USA Today* or following your Facebook friends than you spend in the pursuit to know your Lord, how can you expect God to bless your family relationships to their fullest? Subordinating Christ to the trivial pursuits of the world is a satanic trap. John wrote in his first letter: *"Do not love the world or the things in the world. If anyone loves the world, the love of the Father is not in him. For all that is in the world—the lust of the flesh, the lust of the eyes, and the pride of life—is not of the Father but is of the world. And the world is passing away, and the lust of it; but he who does the will of God abides forever"* (1 John 2:15–17).

God's own words concerning the decision to put Him first are very clear in this outstanding and exciting promise: *"For those who honor Me I will honor, and those who despise Me shall be lightly esteemed"* (1 Sam. 2:30).

Start in Your Own Jerusalem

I know leaders with wrecked home lives who go on mission trips around the world to help others. I have met many who spend more time coaching an employee at work than they do playing games with their son or daughter. These hypocrites are more polite to a stranger than they are to their spouse. Even worse, they keep more commitments to clients than they do to their kids.

In Luke 24:49, right before Jesus ascended into the heavens after His resurrection, He gave these final words to His disciples:

"Behold, I send the Promise of My Father upon you; but tarry in the city of Jerusalem until you are endued with power from on high."

As a result of Jesus's order, a group of about 120 people, including the disciples, stayed in Jerusalem for 10 days until the Holy Spirit came upon them with power for the special ministry of establishing the church. The contingencies that were required of them in order to receive that anointing of the Holy Spirit are also applicable for us today.

First, they followed Christ's strategy by beginning in Jerusalem. *"But you shall receive power when the Holy Spirit has come upon you; and you shall be witness to Me in Jerusalem, and in all Judea and Samaria, and to the end of the earth"* (Acts 1:8). Jerusalem was to be the home base of the church, and God wanted His power to be demonstrated at this home before His followers went to all other nations.

Your "Jerusalem" is your family and community—often the hardest places to live for God. The people who know you best do not expect powerful things to come from you. Even Jesus experienced this and said, *"A prophet is not without honor, but in his own country, and among his own kin, and in his own house"* (Mark 6:4) (Gothard 2005). But you do not need to work miracles, heal the sick, cast out demons, or raise the dead to impress and impact your family. What they need from you is the love and priority that can only come from a heart that loves, prioritizes, and obeys God first.

My wife, Rhonda, and I are in our third decade of marriage. One of our daily joys is to journey through the entire Bible together each year with a structured software program provided by LivingChristian.net. As we put God first each day, our love for Him, for one another, and for other people continues to grow. Consequently, so does our business.

Men, let us revisit the special instructions for you in Ephesians in the light of now knowing that you are to exhibit true leadership by starting in "your own Jerusalem": *"Husbands, love your wives, just as Christ also loved the church and gave Himself for her, that He might sanctify and cleanse her with the washing of the water by the word . . ."* (Eph. 5:25–26).

Paul is telling husbands to cleanse their wives with the "washing of the water by the word"—in other words, to start their spiritual leadership in their own home with their family. This verse does not mean to "get your wife to read the Bible," or even to read it to her. It means to cleanse your own heart and soul by engrafting the pure Word of God into it. Jesus affirmed this meaning when He prayed in John 17:19, *"And for their sakes I sanctify myself, that they also might be sanctified through the truth."* If Jesus sanctified Himself through the truth for our sakes, how much more should we do it for those who are under our spiritual care? (Gothard 2005).

THE DEMON HAD IT RIGHT BUT WAS WRONG

One of the most accurate verses ever recorded in Scripture is Mark 1:24: *"I know who You are—the Holy One of God!"* Yet Jesus rebuked the speaker because it was a demon. There is no clearer evidence that Jesus does not acclaim, but rebukes, those who know who He is but fail to love, trust, and obey Him. When you seek first to know Him, love Him, and obey His Word, THE BOOK promises that "all these things will be added to you," that you will bear fruit, and that Christ will manifest Himself to you.

If you are serious about getting to know God more intimately so that you can obey him more completely, subscribe to the Daily Success Commands of Christ e-mail course from the Institute of Basic Life Principles. It is a 49-week program to help you learn and apply the 49 general commands of Christ. You will receive a brief e-mail lesson daily that helps you know and apply each command. Visit www.iblp.org to register. It is free!

In *How to Run Your Business by THE BOOK*, I included a chapter on life balance and pointed out four key sectors where you must pursue balance: mental, emotional, physical, and spiritual. I mentioned there, and repeat here, that spiritual balance—putting God first—is the foundation that makes the other areas of balance possible and relevant.

By now, I am sure that you see that the secret to work-life balance is simple: There is no secret! The Bible makes clear what you must do, and now you know what it is—but you cannot expect to be blessed until you do it!

PARTING SHOT

This chapter has not been intended to give you the impression that putting God first in your life and surrendering to Him will eliminate your problems at home, at work, and in life and that you will magically find yourself in perfect work-life balance. There will always be trials and temptations that afford you the opportunity to strengthen your faith and forge your character. However, you can be assured that when you follow the steps outlined in this chapter, you will never face these trials alone, or have to get through them on your own strength, using your own wisdom. *That* makes the difference between going through crises fearful and depressed or courageously and with peace.

Omega

"Let your fountain be blessed and rejoice with the wife of your youth" (Prov. 5:18).

1. What is your plan to know God better?
2. Have there been times when troubles at home have made you less effective on the job? In what areas must you become more obedient to God's Word so that your troubles at home are lessened?

"Husbands, likewise, dwell with them with understanding, giving honor to the wife as to the weaker vessel, and as being heirs together of the grace of life, that your prayers may not be hindered (1 Peter 3:7).

What Are Two of the Most Dangerous Mistakes I Must Avoid to Become a More Effective Leader?

Man's Wisdom and Way

Leadership brings pressures that will cause you to make mistakes. No one expects you to be perfect. If you fall short, ask forgiveness. When you commit leadership errors, learn from them. The bottom line is that, since everyone makes their own share of blunders, yours are none of their business.

If you believe the veracity of "Man's Wisdom and Way," please reread Chapter 2, and pay more attention this time! As a leader, your mistakes are everyone's business, because your actions have a greater impact on the culture, morale, momentum, and organizational results than any one else's. You also have the responsibility of setting a righteous example for followers. To appreciate your influence on their behavior, you must grasp that any positive actions you take in abundance, followers will emulate only in moderation. However, any negative actions you initiate in moderation, your followers will imitate in excess. You also accrue a bad reputation and encourage further cultural corruption when your own words and deeds are inconsistent. Sir Francis Bacon explained it well: "He that gives good admonition and bad example builds with one hand and pulls down with the other."

THE BOOK's WISDOM AND WAY

You are not expected to be perfect. But you should strive toward imitating a perfect Lord and Savior as you are instructed in Ephesians 5:1: *"Therefore be imitators of God."* Many leaders use the fact that they cannot become perfect human beings as license to stop striving.

As a leader, you are expected to do more than grow old; you are presumed to grow up and minimize your errors, correct your mistakes, and respond to a misstep backward with a steady gait forward.

Leaders face many temptations and often fall into common traps that affect their character and performance. Loose morals, lousy judgment, outright ignorance, and blatant stupidity are the culprits behind most failures. However, one primary perpetrator underlies each of these causes: pride. In *How to Run Your Business by THE BOOK*, I devoted an entire chapter to explaining how pride is the number one cause of leadership failure. Suffice it to say that if you struggle with either of the two common leadership mistakes I mention in this chapter, pride is at the root of your problem. If you suddenly became defensive or defiant in the face of my accusation that you may have a problem with pride, it is certain evidence that you are guilty as charged.

DANGEROUS MISTAKE #1: PUTTING "PIGS" BEFORE PEOPLE

A common temptation for result-driven leaders is to put more importance on profits than on people, or to regard the material as more valuable than another's humanity. Most leaders would deny that this describes them, yet their actions contradict their assertion. They spend far more time with stuff than with people: reading and writing reports, or engaging in a host of technological distractions that renders the teammates in their own workplace as leadership orphans.

In some ways, many leaders have hearts reminiscent of the townspeople in the Gadarenes region of Galilee in Christ's day. Matthew 8 tells us that Jesus had just crossed the Sea of Galilee and entered this region when He was soon met by two exceedingly fierce demon-possessed men coming out of the tombs. Verse 29 states they cried out in protest against His jurisdiction, *"What have we to do with You, Jesus, You Son of God? Have you come here to torment us before the time?"* Incidentally, their knowledge of Christ proves that it is not knowledge, but love that distinguishes the devils' from Christ's own elect. In fact, it is a true son of hell that knows Christ yet hates Him and will not subject himself to Him.

The book of Luke reports that one of the demons declared his name was "Legion," because there were so many spirits possessing the man. In Roman times, a legion consisted of between 3,000 and

6,000 men! Rather than putting the man through the excruciating process of casting out a legion of demons, Jesus assented to the demon's plea that they be allowed to go into a nearby herd of pigs. On Christ's command of *"Go,"* the demons entered the herd, causing them to run violently down the mountain, into the Sea of Galilee, where they drowned.

What happens next proves that today, just as was true 2,000 years ago, the more you love money, the less you love people. Take a look.

Matthew reports that, irrespective of the fact that the entire town had been told of the miracle of these two tormented souls being delivered from their hell on earth, their apparent preference for pigs caused the townspeople to beg Jesus to depart from their region. This despite the fact that as Jews they should not have had anything to do with herds of ham steaks in the first place! Nor did they express gratitude toward Jesus for commanding the demons into the pigs rather than allowing them to roam the Gadarenes countryside in search of human hosts. Incredibly, these selfish fiends did not even value people enough to bring their sick to Jesus for healing while He was in their neighborhood. Rather, they essentially borrowed the words of the demons themselves, "What have we to do with you, Jesus, Son of God," and they asked that He exit their coast, showing a preference for swine over their Savior. Jesus did not argue with them, and there is no record of Him ever returning to this region. Rejected but not dejected, He boated back to His city of Capernaum, where, in short order, he went on a roll and performed five successive miracles, as described in Matthew 9:

1. He healed a paralytic.
2. He healed a woman who had been bleeding for 12 years.
3. He restored a dead girl to life.

4. He healed two blind men.
5. He healed a mute man by casting out his demon.

One key lesson here is clear: When you devalue people by prioritizing pigs above them, you lose the presence of Christ and the blessings that come with Him. In fact, Jesus is not likely to be welcome in places where pigs, profits, or prizes are esteemed more highly than people whom He loves and made in His image. The "pigs" that come between leaders and people at work and at home today go beyond profits and prizes. They include online poker, BlackBerrys, 500 TV channels, sports, iPads, Internet adultery, social media outlets, and more.

As a leader, you must put people before profits. Profits are fleeting, whereas people are your most appreciable assets. If you prioritize building people over chasing profits, the profits will eventually chase you. This is because the team you have developed and built will reward your investment with new levels of success and results.

You may wish to review the 12 items that comprise a servant-leader's job description in Chapter 3, as these duties ensure that you remain purposeful in your prioritization of people, and they guard you from the perfidious practice of placing your own version of ham hocks ahead of humans.

PRIDE AT THE CORE

How can we blame pride for causing a leader to prioritize pigs over people? Frankly, the only way you could possibly degrade people in the manner exhibited by the citizens of the Gadarenes is to elevate your own selfish welfare onto a pedestal of such heights that the value and dreams of others are completely marginalized. When stripped to its core, human behavior that ostensibly appears as mere indifference or apathy manifests purely as pride at its core, for only an unduly high opinion of self could permit such savage disregard for the welfare of others.

DANGEROUS MISTAKE #2: BECOMING TOO DEPENDENT ON YOURSELF

In my first management job, long before I had ever read a leadership book or attended a business seminar, I had a corrupt understanding of leadership. I believed that the more work I could personally accomplish was evidence of my leadership prowess. I assumed that making my team members dependent on me for directives, ideas, and solutions was healthy. I deduced that because things fell apart in my department whenever I took a day off or went on vacation, it proved my value while I was on the job. Since those early years, I have learned three truths concerning my aberrant assumptions about leadership:

1. The true measure of leaders is not how much they can do personally; rather, it is the ability to get work done through others that marks effective leadership. This is because what one person can do is finite, but what a team can accomplish together has no limits.

2. The true measure of leaders is the ability, over time, to make their teams less dependent on them for direction, ideas, and solutions. Leaders achieve this result by setting clear expectations, pushing power and discretion down the line, and making a conscious effort to develop the skills, talents, and character of each team member.

3. The true measure of leaders is not how well their team members perform while those leaders are present in the workplace applying pressure. Instead, it is adjudged by how well the teams perform in the absence of their leaders.

In his letter to the Ephesians, Paul explained it well by stating that we are to equip others to do the work, not do it all ourselves: *"And He Himself gave some to be apostles, some prophets, some evangelists, and some pastors and teachers, for the equipping of the saints for the work of the ministry . . ."* (Eph. 4:12).

JETHRO TO THE RESCUE

"Thank God for father-in-laws!" That is what Moses must have thought when Jethro gave him priceless advice that would help liberate him from the bondage of making the people of Israel too dependent on him, allowing both Moses and the people to grow toward their fullest potential.

> And so it was, on the next day, that Moses sat to judge the people; and the people stood before Moses from morning until evening. So when Moses' father-in-law saw all that he did for the people, had said, "What is this thing that you are doing for the people? Why do you alone sit and all the people stand before you from morning until evening?" And Moses said to his father-in-law, "Because the people come to me to inquire of God. When they have a difficulty, they come to me, and I judge between one and another; and I make known the statutes of God and His laws." So Moses' father-in-law said to him, "The thing that you do is not good. Both you and these people who are with you will surely wear yourselves out. For this thing is too much for you; you are not able to perform it by yourself." [Exod. 18:13–18]

Did you catch the point Jethro was making? Being a one-man show wears out both leaders and those under their care. Take a look at what Jethro recommended and determine how you can apply the same principle:

> Listen now to my voice: I will give you counsel, and God will be with you: Stand before God for the people, so that you may bring the difficulties to God. And you shall teach them the statutes and the laws, and show them the way in which they must walk and the work they must do. Moreover you shall select from all the people able men, such as fear God, men of truth, hating covetousness; and place such over them to be rulers of thousands, rulers of hundreds, rulers of fifties, and rulers of tens. And let them judge the people at all times. Then it will be that every great matter they shall bring to you, every small matter they themselves will judge. So it will be easier for you, for they will bear the burden with you. If you do this thing, and God so commands you, then you will be able to endure, and all this people will also go to their place in peace. [Exod. 18:19–23]

Note these four key points concerning Jethro's advice that you can apply to your own leadership:

1. Choose people carefully. Clear character criteria were given. Moses was to teach what he knew about God's laws and statutes to others, educating and empowering them to act. Thus, his authority would flow like a river rather than being centralized like a reservoir.
2. Not everyone on the team would have equal responsibility. Some would rule thousands, and others tens.
3. Moses would then be at a point where he would judge only the great matters, making all people less dependent on him.

At the same time, it would allow him to develop other leaders to share his burden and move the welfare of the organization forward.

4. By building a team, Moses would be able to personally endure the rigors of his position, while his people went their way in peace.

MOSES' INNER CIRCLE

In *How to Run Your Business by THE BOOK,* I included a chapter titled, "How to Build a Team by THE BOOK." I highlighted how Jesus had built an inner circle of three key disciples from among his 12 primary team members. Every leader needs an inner circle. Even a small team needs at least one key like-minded and competent go-to person on whom the leader can depend totally.

The seventeenth and eighteenth chapters of Exodus give a unique profile of what a leader's inner circle should look like. The Israelites were on their way to Mount Sinai when the pesky descendants of Esau, the Amalekites, spoiled for a fight. The verses that describe the battle and its aftermath paint a picture of four leaders Moses depended upon to move his team forward.

Aaron and Hur

Aaron was the brother of Moses, and Hur was a prominent official in Israel. As the battle with the Amalekites raged, Moses watched from a hilltop and held the rod of God in his hand. As long as he held the rod upright, Israel prevailed; when he let down his hand, Amalek prevailed. THE BOOK tells that in the midst of the battle, Aaron and Hur stood on separate sides of Moses and supported his hands until the battle was won.

Do you have an Aaron and Hur who are at your side in the midst of your daily battles, supporting you and staying with you to see the fight to a finish? Will they remain with you when things get hot, even if the tide turns against you? I can assure you that in tough times, you cannot do it alone. You need an Aaron and a Hur. The Ecclesiastes writer puts it well: *"Two are better than one. Because they have a good reward for their labor. For if they fall, one will lift up his companion. But woe to him who is alone when he falls. For he has no one to help him up. Again, if two lie down together, they will keep warm. But how can one be warm alone? Though one may be overpowered by another, two can withstand him. And a threefold cord is not quickly broken"* (Eccles. 4:9–12).

Joshua

Moses charged Joshua with choosing the men who would fight in the battle. Joshua followed orders. He got in the trenches, did the dirty work, and defeated the Amalekites.

Where is your Joshua? Who is your go-to person, the one who gets it done, on time and without excuses? This is the same person who covers your back when you take a day off or go on vacation. This is someone you trust, invest in, and reward with additional responsibilities. In today's climate you need fighters, people who are both willing and able to slug it out for the betterment of the organization.

Jethro

The Bible says that, to his credit, Moses heeded his father-in-law's advice and did all that he had told him to. Do you have a Jethro on your team? Consider these three questions:

1. Who, on your team, feels secure enough to give you advice, correct your course and help you erase your blind spots?
2. Do you listen to the feedback when you receive it?
3. Better yet, do you seek out feedback rather than passively wait for it?

The higher you climb on the leadership ladder, the more likely you are to become isolated and aloof, shutting yourself off from the feedback and advice that can enhance or save your career. Do not look at the Jethros in your organization as troublemakers! Consider them instead as corporate activists who care enough about you and the organization to confront you when they feel that you can do better.

PRIDE AT THE CORE

How can we blame pride for a leader's failure to build a team and develop an inner circle? Consider these five reasons:

1. Prideful, insecure leaders will not give up authority or empower others. They hoard it in order to make themselves more powerful and to appear indispensable.
2. Prideful, insecure leaders do not think anyone else can do what they do as well as they do it. Thus, they hang onto tasks rather than training others to do them and then trusting in their abilities.
3. Prideful, insecure leaders do not rely on others, because they do not see the need for others. They reason that as long as they are at the helm, everything will be fine. Everyone else just needs to line up behind them and let them hog the spotlight and run the show.
4. Prideful, insecure leaders will not permit others to get close to them because they may discover their faults and vulnerabilities.
5. Excessive confidence in oneself is proof of pride. James and John wrongly affirmed to Jesus that they were ready to drink from His cup, and Peter adamantly boasted that he would never betray Christ, only to be indicted and shamed by six of the saddest words in the entire Bible, as

145

Mark describes their actions in the immediate aftermath of Jesus's arrest in Gethsemane: *"They all forsook him and fled"* (Mark 14:50).

There is no clearer evidence that pride shreds even the strongest person's will than the abhorrent fact that, in a quest to preserve themselves, all three members of Christ's inner circle turned tail and ran when things got tough in the garden.

The best antidote to pride is to cultivate the humility of Jesus or Moses, of whom it was written: *"Now the man Moses was very humble, more than all men who were on the face of the earth"* (Num. 12:3).

When preparing to journey toward the Promised Land, while speaking to God, Moses uttered profound and humble words worthy of memorization and application by all leaders as they progress on their leadership journey: *"Then he said to Him, 'If Your Presence does not go with us, do not bring us up from here'"* (Exod. 33:15).

NOT SO FAST!

Carefully read the following words of Paul to Timothy when giving guidelines for promoting others into leadership positions: *"Some men's sins are clearly evident, preceding them to judgment, but those of some men follow later. Likewise, the good works of some are clearly evident, and those that are otherwise cannot be hidden"* (1 Tim. 5:24–25).

It is a big mistake to quickly promote newcomers to your organization into leadership positions or to invite them into your inner circle. Paul made the reason very clear. Some team member's sins, faults, and shortcomings are obvious, but the flaws of others "trail behind them." We do not recognize their flaws until they have been around a while.

In the same way, the good deeds of some are obvious—but many outstanding qualities of others are recognized only after long acquaintance. Never make an emotional decision when hiring or promoting someone into leadership. I can promise you that if you wrongly hire or promote people with speed, cleaning up the mess after you realize your mistake and have to replace them is an excruciatingly slow ordeal.

CLOSE THE GAP BETWEEN KNOWING AND DOING

Even if you grasp the importance of empowering others, making them less dependent on you, and mentoring an inner circle, you should not mistake a clear view for a short distance. The work involved in building a team takes lots of time and resources. You will need to perform the following actions, many of which are addressed in this book:

1. Select the right people in the first place. You must hire those who give you character and talent to develop. You can help people become more than they are, but you cannot make them something they are not.
2. Create a strong culture for them to flourish in. This includes clear core values and performance expectations, a bold mission, and an inspiring vision.
3. You must systematically train and coach them to develop their skills and maximize their gifts. Human beings develop to their potential in structured environments, not when they are allowed to drift each day.
4. Insist on accountability. This includes offering fast feedback on their performance and appropriate consequences for both success and failure.
5. Exhibit great leadership to emulate. This is your responsibility, and if you fail to deliver, you fail, period.

As this chapter closes, consider the connection between the two dangerous mistakes listed:

1. Putting "pigs" before people
2. Becoming too dependent on yourself

When you prioritize people over pigs (in whatever form they take), you will be building relationships with team members and investing in their growth. As a natural consequence, you will construct a team that lightens your load and makes you less dependent on yourself. However, falling into the trap of putting pigs before people naturally leads you into the latter error.

OMEGA

"So Moses arose with his assistant Joshua, and Moses went up to the mountain of God. And he said to the elders, 'Wait here for us until we come back to you. Indeed, Aaron and Hur are with you. If any man has a difficulty; let him go to them'" (Exod. 24:13–14).

1. What adjustment must you make in your daily routine to demonstrate that you value your people ahead of your pigs?
2. What, specifically, can you do to make your key people less dependent on you so that you and they may grow?

"And the things that you have heard from me among many witnesses, commit these to faithful men who will be able to teach others also" (2 Tim. 2:2).

How Can I Create More Productive Behaviors in My Organization?

Man's Wisdom and Way

The fastest way to wake up and shake up behaviors in an organization is to change the vision. New visions inspire and unite the team. Vision is a leader's greatest weapon.

I've seen more well-intentioned, energetic leaders take over a new organization, cast their bold new vision, and . . . nothing happens. It falls flat. Nothing changes. No one cares. The leader fails.

THE BOOK's Wisdom and Way

You rarely change behaviors in an organization, measurably or sustainably, by changing its vision. Rather, you change behaviors in an organization by changing the culture. In an already strong culture, vision will accelerate, enhance and focus behaviors. But in a stagnant or struggling enterprise, you cannot effect lasting, substantial change without first strengthening or transforming the culture.

Throughout the Old Testament, God had laid out a vision for His chosen people—how they were to live, worship, and conduct their affairs with others. Because of their sinful hearts and inconsistent leaders, they persisted in behaviors that continually provoked God's wrath. The Old Testament concluded with the book of Malachi, a curse, and a 400-year wait before the Israelites would hear from God through another prophet. When the prophet appeared in the form of John the Baptist, he did not announce a new vision for God's people, but rather the coming of a Leader, Jesus Christ, who would establish a new culture. From that culture would evolve a new mission and vision that would affect and impact every corner of the earth.

THE NEW TESTAMENT CULTURE

After thousands of years of being frustrated by His stiff-necked chosen ones, the last thing God needed to bother with was a new vision for His wayward people to rally around. He intended to rebuild the culture, His earth, by sending a Leader of whom John the Baptist declared: *"I indeed baptize you with water unto repentance, but He who is coming after me is mightier than I, whose sandals I am not worthy to carry. He will baptize you with the Holy Spirit and fire. His winnowing fan is in His hand, and He will thoroughly clean out His threshing floor, and gather His wheat into the barn, but He will burn up the chaff with unquenchable fire"* (Matt. 3:11–12).

Notice also that John quoted passages in Isaiah that portended both a new Leader and a new culture: *"The voice of one crying in the wilderness; 'Prepare the way of the Lord; make His paths straight. Every valley shall be filled and every mountain and hill brought low; the crooked places shall be made straight and the rough ways smooth; and all flesh shall see the salvation of God'"* (Luke 3:4–6).

After Jesus's three-plus years of ministry, healing, teaching, and living by example, He was crucified. He had changed the culture in a manner that would create the behaviors necessary to support the vision He had cast to His disciples in Matthew 28:19: *"Go therefore and make disciples of all nations, baptizing them in the name of the Father and of the Son and of the Holy Spirit, teaching them to observe all things that I have commanded you . . ."*

These two passages, one lengthy and one brief, from the book of Acts resolutely address His success in this mission:

> And with many other words he [Peter] testified and exhorted them, saying, "Be saved from this perverse generation." Then those who gladly received his word were baptized: and that day about three thousand souls were added to them. And they continued steadfastly in the apostles' doctrine and fellowship, in the breaking of bread, and in prayers. Then fear came up on every soul, and many wonders and signs were done through the apostles. Now all who believed were together, and had all things in common, and sold their possessions and goods, and divided them among all, as anyone had need. So continuing daily with one accord in the temple, and breaking bread from house to house, they ate their

151

food with gladness and simplicity of heart, praising God and having favor with all the people. And
the Lord added to the church daily those who were
being saved. [Acts 2:40–47]

These who have turned the world upside down
have come here too. [Acts 17:6]

CULTURE'S FIVE PRIMARY COMPONENTS

While many factors contribute to an organization's culture, the
following five are the most significant and defining components:

1. *Core values.* In Chapter 9, I presented our own five corporate core values, six benefits of core values, and seven sample values established by Jesus during His Sermon on the
   Mount. Without question, core values shape the foundation
   of any organization, just as character determines the foundation of any individual. And just as your character will
   influence your personal choices and actions, an organization's culture will dictate the behaviors within its walls.

2. *Mission.* In Chapter 9, I defined mission as purpose. Your
   mission statement must answer the question, "Why do we
   exist as an organization?" While Jesus began presenting His
   core values during His Sermon on the Mount as recorded
   in Matthew 5–7, He declared His purpose on earth in Mark
   10:45: *"For even the Son of Man did not come to be served, but to
   serve, and to give His life a ransom for many."*

3. *Performance standards.* While core values are character-
   based behaviors, performance standards are benchmarks
   for accomplishing the technical aspects of one's job with
   excellence. A high-performance culture has high standards
   for both behavioral and technical performance. Creating

clear guidelines for core values, mission, and performance standards also provides a guideline for accountability—a guideline essential for the sustenance of robust culture. In Matthew 10, Jesus sent out the 12 disciples with clear, specific, and high standards for performing the technical aspects of their ministry:

> These twelve Jesus sent out and commanded them saying: "Do not go into the way of the Gentiles, and do not enter a city of the Samaritans. But go rather to the lost sheep of the house of Israel. And as you go, preach, saying, 'The kingdom of heaven is at hand.' Heal the sick, cleanse the lepers, raise the dead, cast out demons. Freely you have received, freely give. Provide neither gold nor silver nor copper in your money belts, nor bag for your journey, not two tunics, nor sandals, nor staffs; for a worker is worthy of his food. Now whatever city or town you enter, inquire who in it is worthy, and stay there until you go out. And when you go into a household, greet it. If the household is worthy, let your peace come upon it. But if it is not worthy, let your peace return to you. And whoever will not receive you nor hear your words, when you depart from that house or city, shake off the dust from your feet." [Matt. 10:5–15]

4. *Core competencies.* Core competencies are the strongest abilities of your organization. They are the aspects a competitor or outsider would look at and muse, "I wish we did X as well as they do." Core competencies help create your unique brand; they make you different, better, and excellent. Your talent and financial resources must align with and fuel

your core competencies in order to consistently grow your enterprise. If you aspire to be great, you must eventually shift your focus from doing many tasks well to doing fewer things with greater excellence. Those few things are enabled and leveraged by and through your core competencies.

Even more important than having core competencies per se is having core competencies that are relevant to achieving your vision. For example, an automobile manufacturer that aspires to build the world's best cars yet is staffed with the world's best plumbers has created a hopeless situation where the culture and vision are severely out of alignment. In fact, mismatches like this will diminish the culture and marginalize the vision.

Early in Christ's ministry, He established what the culture-supporting core competency would be for His ministry. While many would say that healing and miracles were His primary core competency, Jesus saw it differently. He knew that healings and miracles could affect the outer person, but He had come to change the inner person, and thus He gave greater priority to this end:

At evening, when the sun had set, they brought to Him all who were sick and those who were demon-possessed. And the whole city was gathered together at the door. Then He healed many who were sick with various diseases, and cast out many demons; and He did not allow the demons to speak because they knew Him. Now in the morning, having risen a long while before daylight, He went out and departed to a solitary place; and there He prayed. And Simon and those who were with Him searched for Him. When they found Him, they said to Him, "Everyone is looking for You." [They naturally wanted an encore performance from the healing show of the night before.] But He said to them, "Let us go into the next towns, that I may preach there also, because for this purpose I have come forth." [This reinforced His mission: to serve and not be served and to give His life as a ransom for many, as it was His preaching and not His healings and miracles that created the basis for charges to be brought against Him.] And He was preaching in their synagogues throughout all Galilee, and casting out demons. [Mark 1:32–39]

It is important to note at this point how masterfully Jesus's mission, core values, performance expectations, and core competencies all aligned with and supported His ultimate vision. He left an incredible organizational model to emulate.

5. *People.* Based on the cultural components discussed thus far, it is obvious that Jesus was building a culture that would attract and develop people who would:
- Put God and others first in their lives.
- Reconcile and forgive quickly to keep relationships strong.
- Gladly serve others and go the second mile.
- Trade in worry for faith in Him.
- Share the Gospel with others and teach them the way.
- Love those who persecuted them.
- Live in a manner that would serve as light, drawing others to Christ and out of the darkness.

Christ sought teachable, not perfect, people to join His culture. Heart would matter more than status, education, credentials, or riches. He created behavioral and performance standards even higher than those established in Old Testament law. But He did so knowing that those who truly loved Him would aspire to that standard, not out of duty or legalism, but because they sought His fellowship, presence, and approval.

The collection of core values, mission, performance standards, core competencies, and people forges a culture that changes behavior; this is not the question. The question is, what is the quality of your five primary culture components, and which behaviors are you seeing as a result? If they are not what you desire, do not expect to significantly alter behaviors by launching a new vision, giving a polished pep talk, or rolling out a new contest, incentive, or threat. If I may boldly, and not so gently, remind you why this is true, here is what is important to remember and repeat lovingly to yourself whenever you are tempted to apply those tactics as your first order of business to change behaviors in your organization: "It's the culture, stupid!"

Chief Architect and Primary Influencer

The chief architect and primary influencer is, of course, the leader. A culture is very unlikely to change much unless one of two things occurs:

1. The leader changes.
2. The leader is changed.

Oftentimes, item 2 is necessary because item 1 does not happen.

I enjoy watching professional football. My favorite team once fell into a deep slump during which they had won only one game and lost seven. Unveiling a new vision for the team to "win the rest of their games" would not have changed a thing. Rather, they needed a culture change, and fast. The shortest, surest way to change a culture in this case was option 2: The team's owners changed the coach. In the ensuing weeks, here is how the sports press categorized the changes made by the new coach:

- Players were required to begin showing up on time for practices (values and performance standards).
- Players were required to once again adhere to the dress code for travel days (values and performance standards).
- The team would get back to doing what they did best and build on that foundation. In this case, it was returning to their running game (core competencies).
- The team would begin practicing harder, using full pads during the week (performance standards).
- Players would be more harshly measured by their effort, and those not giving all would be benched (people).
- The team focused on making each day great, including the practices. Their new mantra: "We will be great today" (mission).

This coach is rebuilding his foundation—his team's culture. Once it is strengthened and sound, he can credibly begin speaking in terms of vision.

Incidentally, even though the season seemed hopeless only halfway through the year, the week after the new coach took over, the team started winning again. While their record was 1–7 for the first 8 games, they won 5 of their final 8 games.

DRASTIC ACTION IS SOMETIMES REQUIRED

Occasionally, a culture has devolved to the point where the organization cannot, or should not, be saved. In other words, it has reached the point at which no leader, set of values, mission, standards, competencies, or group of people can turn things around. In this case, it is better to fold up the tents, clean house, and either start over or move on to something with higher upward potential. Or, if you are God, you send a flood. *Adam's Synchronological Chart* lists a gap of 1,656 years between the Creation and Noah's deluge. In that period of time, humankind had behaved in a manner that provoked one of the saddest passages in THE BOOK, as recorded in Genesis 6:5–7: *"Then the Lord saw that the wickedness of man was great in the earth, and that every intent of the thoughts of his heart was only evil continually. And the Lord was sorry that He had made man on the earth, and He was grieved in His heart. So the Lord said, 'I will destroy man whom I have created from the face of the earth, both man, and beast, creeping thing, and birds of the air, for I am sorry that I have made them.'"*

Twelve chapters, or 450 years, after the Flood in Genesis 18, God decided that the grave sin and corrupt culture of Sodom and Gomorrah warranted obliteration, and He destroyed them with a barrage of fire and brimstone. As Jude described centuries later:

> But I want to remind you, though you once knew
> this, that the Lord, having saved the people out of the
> land of Egypt, afterward destroyed those who did not
> believe. And the angels who did not keep their proper
> domain, but left their own abode. He has reserved in
> everlasting chains under darkness, for the judgment
> of the great day; as Sodom and Gomorrah, and the
> cities around them in a similar manner to these having
> given themselves over to sexual immorality and gone
> after strange flesh, are set forth as an example, suffer-
> ing the vengeance of eternal fire. [Jude 5–7]

A new vision, pep talk, or incentive program wasn't going to save Sodom and Gomorrah. The culture had become toxic beyond repair. Lesson for your organization: Do not wait for the bottom to fall out before you begin strengthening your culture. You probably have less time than you think.

BE A STUDENT OF BEHAVIORS

You cannot lead effectively if you confuse the scoreboard for the game, becoming obsessed with numbers while you ignore daily behaviors within your culture. Yet many leaders pride themselves as astute students of numbers. Instead, they should become students of behaviors, because the behaviors serve as an MRI of your culture and portend where the numbers are headed.

In case you have missed it: The numbers in your organization are a result of the culture! This is because culture dictates behaviors, and behaviors determine results. By carefully watching the daily behaviors of your people, you can intervene to strengthen the culture and alter behaviors before the numbers show up. On the other hand, if you are watching only for the numbers, all you are seeing are the lagging indicators. Numbers show up too late to change anything. If all you are doing is gazing at the scoreboard, you are missing the game—and the opportunity to influence the behaviors within the game that determine what goes up on the scoreboard.

When you study behaviors within your organization, you can effectively predict the future. The daily behaviors of your people will tell you exactly where the numbers are headed. In fact, wherever you are today results from the culture-induced behaviors of the past. Where you will be in the future will result from the culture-induced behaviors taking place in your organization at this very moment.

Change Culture with Addition or Subtraction

The arrival of Jesus and His teachings was the catalyst for creating the Christian culture. Likewise, in your own organization, you can often change a culture by who you add to it. Unfortunately not all additions bring value to the culture; some instead diminish it, which lends increased importance to the three chapters on hiring strategies earlier in this book.

You can also change a culture by who you remove from it. When King David was on his deathbed, his desire was for his heir, Solomon, to rule in peace so that he could complete the work of building the Temple. Thus, David gave orders to clean up a few cultural messes, potential culture cancers, that could inhibit the new king's success. In short order, David ordered a Mafia-style hit on the disloyal commander Joab and on the troublemaker Shimei. Solomon also eliminated his traitorous brother Adonijah and commanded that Abiathar, the priest, be exiled. After the completion of this cultural cleansing, the Bible declares: *"Thus the kingdom was established in the hand of Solomon"* (1 Kings 2:46).

Consequently, Solomon's reign consisted of 40 consecutive years of peace. There is a very good chance that before your own culture can regain solid traction, you will need to perform your own purge of misfits, malcontents, and saboteurs.

You Do Not Have to Be *THE* Leader to Change the Culture

If you are not *the* leader in your organization, that certainly does not mean you cannot positively affect the culture. THE BOOK is filled with examples of individuals, many without official titles at all, who were instrumental in influencing the primary influencers who shaped the culture.

1. Joseph, the former slave, shaped Egyptian culture as Pharaoh's second-in-command (refer to Genesis).
2. Daniel, the one-time captive and eventual governor, shaped Babylonian and Persian cultures under multiple administrations and kings (refer to Daniel).
3. Mordecai's and his cousin Esther's influence on King Xerxes strengthened and preserved the Jewish culture from Haman's plot to annihilate Jews in the 127 provinces, from India to Ethiopia, ruled by Xerxes (refer to Esther).
4. Prophets like Isaiah, Ezekiel, Jeremiah, Amos, and others were men without official titles, power, or rank; however, they shaped their cultures and influenced rulers and followers alike (refer to the books of each namesake).

CHANGE THROUGH ADRENALINE SURGE

It is entirely possible to occasionally cast a bold vision, rally the troops, and effect change through an adrenaline surge within the confines of a weak culture—and to do so without working hard or long to transform that culture. But without a strong foundation in place, behaviors will slide backward, further weakening the culture and making the attainment of future vision objectives unlikely.

Nehemiah, and his urgent effort to rebuild the Jerusalem wall is evidence of this phenomenon. After taking a leave of absence as King Artaxerxes' cupbearer in Babylon for the purpose of rebuilding the protective wall of Jerusalem, Nehemiah arrived and assessed the sad state of Jewish culture in that city. After careful observation, he decided to rally its downtrodden citizens in an effort to rebuild the wall and raise the security level and esteem of its people, while removing the reproach associated with unprotected cities. In Jerusalem's case, this particular black eye had been in evidence for more than 100 years. Nehemiah's focus and leadership as he spearheaded the construction project were incredible, and he and his team completed the job in only 52 days! And they did so without first laying the cultural foundation normally necessary to complete such a task. Intensity, teamwork, excitement, and adrenaline—empowered by the ever-present hand of God—enabled this stunning achievement.

After remaining in Jerusalem for 12 more years, Nehemiah returned to Babylon for a period of time to continue his work for King Artaxerxes. As he departed, he failed to address one of the five key components of culture: putting the right people in leadership positions. Without this essential cultural element in place, Jerusalem experienced firsthand the second law of thermodynamics: Things do not wind up, they wind down, unless energy is applied. Or, as we all learn in life at one time or another, prosperity drains urgency.

The Bible does not tell us how long Nehemiah was away from Jerusalem. It does, however, clearly demonstrate that upon his return he went slightly nuts as he observed how far the culture had fallen in his absence. Here's what he found:

- The men charged with maintaining the temple had not been given their allotment of food and were forced to return home rather than caring for the temple, thus impairing mission, performance standards, people, core values, and core competencies, all in one fell swoop!

- The people profaned the Sabbath, corrupting the culture's values.
- The Jews intermarried with the worst sort of heathen, diminishing a key component of culture.

Nehemiah had to begin whipping the culture back into shape in order to produce behaviors that would be worthy of God's blessing. In his own words, he explains his urgent action: *"So I contended with them and cursed them, struck some of them, pulled out their hair; and made them swear by God saying, 'You shall not give your daughters as wives to their sons, nor take their daughters for your sons of yourselves. Did not Solomon king of Israel sin by these things? Yet among many nations there was no king like him, who was beloved of his God; and God made him king over all Israel. Nevertheless pagan women caused even him to sin'"* (Neh. 13:25–26).

The lesson? Build, strengthen, and protect your culture so that the behaviors emanating from it take you to your vision. Trying to cast vision without the underlying foundation of culture is like endeavoring to build a skyscraper from the top down. You will create a lot of movement and noise, but the result is certain collapse.

OMEGA

"Thus says the Lord of hosts: 'Consider your ways! Go up to the mountains and bring wood and build the temple, that I may take pleasure in it and be glorified,' says the Lord. 'You looked for much, but indeed it came to little; and when you brought it home, I blew it away. Why?' says the Lord of hosts. 'Because of My house that is in ruins, while every one of you runs to his own house. Therefore the heavens above you withhold the dew, and the earth withholds its fruit'" (Hag. 1:7–10).

1. Which of the five cultural components is strongest and which is weakest in your organization?
2. Which behaviors within your culture are currently unacceptable and must be changed in order to strengthen your culture?

"Therefore whoever hears these sayings of Mine, and does them, I will liken him to a wise man who built his house on the rock: and the rain descended, the floods came, and the winds blew and beat on that house; and it did not fall, for it was founded on the rock" (Matt. 7:24–25).

How Do I Know God's Will as I Make Decisions in My Business and Life?

MAN'S WISDOM AND WAY

If your intentions are good and you don't violate God's principles, He will bless your decisions because He wants you to prosper. Besides, what sort of testimony does it offer if a Christian fails in the business world? Use the gifts and talents that God gives you for moral purposes and God will stay on your side. Make a decision, and if you don't feel any inner conflict, God is with you. That's a sign to move forward in faith. As you take the first step, ask God to bless your decision and guide your way.

This self-serving, lazy person's method for discovering God's will in making decisions has gotten a whole lot of folks into a heap of trouble. Those who subscribe to this philosophy are so determined

How to Lead by THE BOOK

to do what *they* want that unless Jesus Himself appears before them brandishing a stop sign, they assume He's on their side.

THE BOOK's Wisdom and Way

Christians commonly take missteps as they mistake faith for presumption. You cannot make godly decisions, nor will you know God's will for anything, until you give up control of your life to Him. Most Christians make decisions about what they want to do and then ask God to bless those decisions. Then later, they plead with Him to bail them out of the consequences of their poor and selfish choices.

If you are waiting to understand what God's will is so you can then decide if you want to participate, you have it backward. Instead, you must commit to what God wants for you, then ask Him to reveal it. The commitment comes before the understanding, because God does not share His will for contemplation but for participation. You should probably not expect Him to reveal His entire "100-step plan" all at once, either. Discipline yourself to be content with your daily bread, and let God reveal what you need to know for the moment, increasing your trust in and dependence on Him.

You will have a far easier time making godly decisions if you know what is in THE BOOK. This is because God's will for your life will never contradict His Word. The Bible acts as a filter for decision making. The more you understand it, the easier it is for you to know what to do and what not to do in a given situation.

It Is about Relationship

While speaking at a conference, a businessman asked me, "How do I hear God's voice in my daily business walk?" These were my answers.

166

The key to hearing God's voice in *anything* is your relationship with Him. You may recall that I first suggested in Chapter 10 that relationship is the key to knowing God and that obedience is the key to that relationship. This connection is essential to good decision making, because the closer your relationship to God, the easier it is to know what He wants and expects from you in every circumstance. However, you cannot develop intimate relationships with people, much less with God, unless you spend sufficient time with them. Sending up an occasional flare prayer when you are desperate does not build a relationship with God. If that is your pattern, then God and you will remain little more than casual acquaintances.

In Chapter 10, I also emphasized the importance of putting God first in your life. Since that specific theme is reinforced also in this chapter, it should now be quite clear that surrender to God is the key to leading at your fullest potential and living a robust life. Many people go through their entire lives and never fully accept or embrace the principles of (1) *relationship* (hearing God's voice), (2) *obedience* (the key to relationship), and (3) *putting God first in your life*, which makes relationship and obedience possible.

Frankly, there is no shortcut around these requirements—no plan B. And for this you should be grateful! The greatest joys in life are the rewards that come from thinking less of yourself and more of God, for people who think the least of themselves are those of whom God thinks the most.

Some people resist coming to God at all, much less wholeheartedly, because they feel unfit and unqualified. But you do not come to God because you are fit; you come precisely because you are unfit. Your unfitness is your fitness. Your qualification is your lack of qualification. Just come in an attitude of surrender, and let God go to work on you and through you.

167

While you may never hear the audible voice of God, you will feel it in your spirit—that still small voice of the Holy Spirit that those who know God come to recognize as an old and trusted friend.

In the second chapter of Acts, the disciples narrowed down the successor of Judas to two candidates. *"And they proposed two: Joseph called Barsabbas, who was surnamed Justus, and Matthias. And they prayed and said, 'You, O Lord, who know the hearts of all, show which of these two You have chosen to take the part of this ministry and apostleship from which Judas by transgressions fell, that he might go to his own place.' And they cast their lots, and the lots fell on Matthias. And he was numbered with the eleven apostles"* (Acts 2:23–26).

Just two verses later, the Holy Spirit was sent and came upon all those gathered in the Upper Room for Pentecost. Because God sent His Spirit to dwell within and guide believers, there is no further record in THE BOOK of any believer having to make a decision by casting lots. The Power Source is within all believers still today, so that is not the question. The question is only whether you seek His guidance in your daily decisions or continue to embrace your own method for "casting lots." The decisions do not need to be major to garner God's attention or gain His interest. Peter reminds us in his Epistle that God cares about the little decisions as well as the biggies. *"Therefore humble yourselves under the mighty hand of God, that He may exalt you in due time, casting all your care upon Him, for He cares for you"* (1 Pet. 5:6–7).

Five BOOK-Based Decisions

God wants you to pray for His guidance for decisions large and small. He wants to share His will with you as much as you want to know it. If you are not hearing from God in this regard, it may indicate one of three possibilities:

1. You have not subordinated your own will to His, and thus you keep getting in your own way.
2. You have not asked Him for guidance or sought counsel from mature Christians or from THE BOOK.
3. You are so far from Him that you cannot recognize His voice.

Yes, God speaks to you as you read the Bible (if you happen to read it), through others (if you are humble enough to listen), and through prayer (if you turn off the television long enough to pray). I want to reiterate here that God will never tell you something that violates His Word or His stated ways as presented throughout THE BOOK. Here are five examples:

1. In the Bible, God tells us to *"owe no man anything other than love"* (Rom. 13:8). Proverbs 22:7 warns, *"The rich rules over the poor, and the borrower is servant to the lender."* Thus, it will never be God who tells you to go into debt. If you go into debt, God may still decide to prosper you, but you will never prosper in the manner that God had planned for you had you loved Him enough to trust Him and obey His Word.
2. Ephesians 4:25 says, *"Therefore putting away all lying, Let each one of you speak truth with his neighbor, for we are members of one another."* This means that it is never God's will for you to lie to anyone about anything. Yes, that also means the "harmless" little white lies. When a Scripture says *all*, it means just that: *every*, excluding none.
3. It is never God's will for you to cheat the tax collector, even if you do not like the government or are protesting that your funds are being used for immoral uses. Romans 13:7 commands: *"Render therefore to all their due: taxes to whom taxes are*

due, customs to whom customers, fear to whom fear, honor to whom honor."

4. You cannot rationalize dishonoring your father and mother. God emphasized the importance of this fifth of the Ten Commandments by making it unique, in that it is the only commandment with a promise: *"Honor your father and your mother, that our days may be long upon the land which the Lord your God is giving you"* (Exod. 20:12).

5. It is not God's will for you to be a legal business partner with a non-Christian. *"Do not be unequally yoked together with unbelievers. For what fellowship has righteousness with lawlessness? And what communion has light with darkness?"* (2 Cor. 6:14).

As you can see, the more that you know and understand God's moral will—His commandments and dos and don'ts—the easier it is for you to know His personal will for you in a given situation.

KNOWLEDGE BRINGS RESPONSIBILITY

It is also important to understand that more responsibility comes with knowing His commands, because you can no longer plead ignorance if you break them! James 4:17 issues a strong warning for those who know what is right but fail to do it: *"Therefore, to him who knows to do good and does not do it, to him it is sin."* This means that you not only sin by doing wrong, but that you also sin by remaining idle and doing nothing versus taking action and doing what is right when you see the opportunity to do so.

GIVE UP TO GO UP

If you spend more spare time with reality television shows, golf courses, partying, texting friends, iPads, or computer games than you do learning more about God or communing with Him, you are probably not hearing from Him too often. Incidentally, it is not because He moved or does not care, it is because you left Him. Zechariah 1:3 offers a great promise in this regard: *"Therefore, say to them, 'Thus says the Lord of hosts: "Return to Me," says the Lord of hosts, "and I will return to you," says the Lord of hosts.'"* Second Chronicles 16:9 promises: *"For the eyes of the Lord run to and fro throughout the whole earth, to show Himself strong on behalf of those whose heart is loyal to Him."*

Learn from the apostle John. His Gospel reveals more intimate details about Christ's life than the others. This is because John was Christ's best friend and stayed very close to Him. Because of his proximity and intimacy, he gained insights that those following at a distance missed. Jesus did not have to shout to get John's attention.

Evaluate your daily routine and determine what you have to give up so that you can go up with God. Start putting God on your schedule first, then work the rest of the day around God, rather than trying to squeeze God into the rest of your day. Making this trade-off will change your life.

If you have an interest in increasing or strengthening the spiritual disciplines in your life so that you come to know God more intimately, I recommend the book *Spiritual Disciplines for the Christian Life* by Donald Whitney. In my entire life, I have read only a handful of books that are as saturated with the level of applicable wisdom and insight as Whitney's.

"All Your Ways" Means *All Your Ways*

Proverbs 3:5–6 offers an outstanding promise for securing God's guidance and knowing His will. There is just one catch. *"Trust in the Lord with all your heart, and lean not on your own understanding; in all your ways acknowledge Him and He shall direct your paths."*

Did you catch the *catch*? It is *"all"* your ways. In other words, you cannot turn parts of your life over to God and keep others under your own control and expect to hear His voice or know His will. Some Christians turn their health, family, and job over to God, but then use their own wisdom when it comes to finances. As a result, they do not tithe, they go into debt, they live beyond their means, and they take on wrong partnerships. Then they appear bewildered about why they are struggling. The answer is simple: Their partial obedience ranks as complete disobedience! God never said, "Acknowledge me in all the ways you are comfortable." Quite simply, *"all your ways,"* means *all* your ways!

THE $60,000 QUESTION

While I was the guest on a call-in radio show to promote *How to Run Your Business by THE BOOK*, a listener asked, in tears, why I thought that God was not blessing her business. She confided that her husband had been at a job where he did not feel appreciated and so was compelled to leave and begin his own repair business. They felt God was leading them in this direction, so they borrowed $60,000 for a shop and equipment. The business struggled from day one, and they were now unable to pay back their loans. Based on the limited information I had, I suggested three possibilities for their struggle:

1. It appeared that rather than seeking God's will, they decided on their own that the husband should leave his job and go into debt; then they asked God to bless their foolishness.
2. It may not have been God's will for her husband to leave his job just because he did not feel appreciated. God may have wanted to use him there to influence others, or to learn humility, or some other lesson that would bring great benefit to his life.

3. They may have heard from someone or something concerning borrowing $60,000 to start their business, but it certainly was not from God (more about this in Chapter 14). God would not lead them to do something that would contradict His Word. He may have wanted them to wait and save the money or to sell certain assets in order to raise the funds. In Matthew 13, Jesus tells two short but important parables in this regard:

- *"Again, the kingdom of heaven is like a treasure hidden in a field, which a man found and hid; and for joy over it he goes and sells all the he has and buys that field"* (Matt. 13:44).
- *"Again, the kingdom of heaven is like a merchant seeking beautiful pearls, who, when he had found one pearl of great price, went and sold all the he had and bought it"* (Matt. 13:45–46).

In neither case did the person take out a loan to get what was of great value. Rather, each one sold current assets. Undoubtedly, either of these characters could have rationalized going in to debt for such worthy treasure, but it would not have aligned with God's Word.

THE KEY TO TIME MANAGEMENT

If you have not actively or consistently sought God's will for the daily decisions you make at home or on the job, then you are probably an ineffective time manager. After all, how can you possibly know whether to say yes or no on a daily basis if you have no clue whether it fits God's will for you?

Following your own wisdom and going with your gut will cause you to major in minor things and minor in the major things. You will be prone to immerse yourself in a swirl of activity each day to hide the fact that you are not sure what you are doing, or if what you are doing is what you should be doing! You probably put in plenty of hours trying to get your work done, but still fall short because you are not focusing enough on what you are putting *in* to all of those hours. Thus, much of the time, you are like an octopus on roller skates—lots of movement but little real progress.

God expects us to be great stewards of the precious time he gives us. Paul offers classic time management advice in Ephesians 5:16: *"See then that you walk circumspectly, not as fools, but as wise, redeeming the time, because the days are evil."*

When you redeem something, you trade it in for something more valuable. This is what you are able to do when you give up what is good for what is great, when you stop being wise in your own eyes and commit all your ways to Him so that He will direct your paths.

The key to time management is not using planners and check-lists. Rather, it is daily seeking God's will for your life. Anything else is just a daily crapshoot.

INCREASE YOUR FOCUS BY FINDING YOUR PASSION

As I conclude this chapter on knowing God's will for your work life, I want to include a principle for discovering God's overreaching purpose for your life overall—that place where you will find the most meaning and fulfillment in exchange for your time here on earth. After all, life consists of far more than simply working and making money. Ultimately, it is about making a difference and becoming significant in your family, church, and the world overall. But becoming significant requires passion, and most folks go about trying to find their passion in a backward manner. Here is what I mean.

As human beings, we long for meaning. Sadly, we often look for it in the wrong places. We conjure up dynamic visions for our lives, and we hope that the vision stirs up our passion, adding meaning and purpose to our existence. In fact, vision has been described as "a picture of the future that produces passion in you." I agree, but if this is how you hope to identify or stir up your passion, then your passion will eventually die out. You see, when passion is created from the outside in, it can cause a momentary flash of emotion, but it will not be enough to move you very far or for very long. As soon as things get tough along your journey, you will slow down, back up, or walk away and look for something else. The embers of passion stirred by your vision will not draw out the tenacity, mental toughness, and resiliency you need to bring your vision to fruition. Instead of embers, you need an inferno of passion to power you and sustain you on your vision quest.

This is why you cannot cast a vision and count on it to create the passion necessary to be successful. Rather, your vision must be birthed from your passion! Did you get that? In order to be effective, vision must come from your passion, rather than hoping your passion will come from a vision. This fact begs the obvious question: Where does one discover this inner passion that so many people never find or tap into? Where does it come from? It comes from where all true passion comes from: It comes from anguish. Leaders like Moses, Nehemiah, Martin Luther King Jr., Mother Teresa, and Nelson Mandela all had bold visions that were birthed from their passion. Their passion was rooted in their anguish. *Anguish* is defined as an "agonizing mental pain or torment brought about by conditions in or around you." What torments you? What keeps you awake at night? What moves you? What burns inside of you? What thoughts, purposes, or dreams consume you? What do you agonize over? What brings you before God in tears? That is where you will find your passion, and that passion will birth your vision.

Do not miss the following fact: It is not enough to be concerned about an issue or a cause. You must anguish over it! Concern creates interest, whereas anguish creates movement and resolve and makes you unstoppable. Stop ignoring your pain and start celebrating your torment—your anguish—and you will tap into the passion that can become the catalyst to your vision, your purpose, and eventually, your legacy.

You may already work in a position where you can address your anguish. For instance, if you anguish over watching others fail to reach their God-given potential and instead live lives of quiet desperation, then determine how you can use this anguish to help those you are responsible for to improve their performance and results. Then pursue ways to pour that passion into the world beyond your home and workplace. Tell Him that you commit to whatever He wants you to do in this regard. Surrender your gifts and passion to Him. Then ask Him to show you how to proceed.

OMEGA

"But as for me, I would seek God, and to God I would commit my cause—Who does great things, and unsearchable, marvelous things without number. . . . He frustrates the devices of the crafty, so that their hands cannot carry out their plans. He catches the wise in their own craftiness and the counsel of the cunning comes quickly upon them" (Job 5:8–9, 12–13).

1. What are your first steps to more actively seeking God's will for your life and in your daily decision making?
2. Have you ever surrendered totally to God and said: "Lord, I'll do it. Now what is it?" Would you benefit by doing this now?

"I know your works, that you are neither cold nor hot. I could wish you were cold or hot. So then, because you are lukewarm, and neither cold nor hot, I will vomit you out of My mouth. Because you say, 'I am rich, have become wealthy, and have need of nothing'—and do not know that you are wretched, miserable, poor, blind, and naked" (Rev. 3:15–17).

What Are the Two Biggest Threats to My Success?

MAN'S WISDOM AND WAY

The business landscape is filled with minefields: aggressive competition, government regulation, economic meltdowns, and the like. These persistent threats are always circling like vultures, looking for an opportunity to devour your organization. To make matters worse, you remain vulnerable to the defection of big clients and top performers. As if that's not enough, you'll really discover what stress is all about the day the bank decides to yank your credit line! A combination of forces like these is what should keep you on your toes and prevent you from ever becoming too comfortable. They loom as the biggest, most persistent threats to your success. What is particularly frustrating about them is that they are beyond your control.

An essential step to maturing as a human being is resisting the temptation to blame conditions beyond your control to explain away your lack of success. It is only by focusing on the aspects of our lives that we can control that we maintain any personal power in our lives. These things include, but are not limited to:

The strength of your relationship with God
Your daily character choices
Your attitude
Where you spend your time
With whom you spend your time
Whether you exercise discipline
Whether you continue to learn and grow
Your work ethic

When you make wise decisions in key areas like these, they will make the outside conditions that besiege you less relevant.

THE BOOK's WISDOM AND WAY

The threats triggered by adverse outside conditions just mentioned in "Man's Wisdom and Way" are genuine. Yet the biggest threats to your organization do not come from the outside; they come from the inside, and they *are* within your control! Far too often, these emanate from within the character flaws of the leaders in charge of the organization. While the impact of adverse outside conditions is important and cannot be ignored, a leader can marginalize the effects of such factors by making the right inside decisions and character choices. On the other hand, poor character decisions by a leader can create a train wreck in their organizations despite outside conditions that are robust and favorable. In order to lead by THE BOOK, you are well advised to focus more on controlling what is in the mirror than on what lies outside the window.

In *How to Run Your Business by THE BOOK*, I addressed character flaws like pride, failing to keep commitments, and failing to forgive. Although I could include here a seemingly endless menu of poor character choices a leader can make that cause personal and organizational self-destruction, this chapter focuses on two major threats to your well-being: (1) sexual immorality and (2) following false teachers and their ungodly counsel.

THE AGE OF "IT'S NO BIG DEAL"

It may be time to reread the preface of this book, as it will help set the stage for this chapter. In the preface I outlined eight evidences of cultural decline and six of its consequences for your organization. Much of what's wrong with the world today can be explained by the new mantra of our overly tolerant society as it responds to sin with the attitude: "It's no big deal." For some people, it seems that no sin is a big deal anymore, despite what THE BOOK says about it. Many in society—including nominal Christians—have lost their fear of, and reverence for, God. They consider THE BOOK as a marginally relevant historical compilation with little genuine application for real-world people living today. THE BOOK might have meant something in its day, but this is a more evolved and enlightened age that demands a contemporary and "realistic" approach to life. Mark my words, you will never successfully combat the two biggest threats presented in this chapter until you acknowledge THE BOOK's contemporary relevance. Only then are you likely to renounce and discard the "It's no big deal" tolerance and defense of sin. This mantra is demonically inspired and will drag to hell those who profess, practice, and promote its legitimacy. While most practitioners of sexual immorality and false teachings may never say the words, "It's no big deal" to excuse their moral failures, their persistence in these pursuits declares it for them.

THE BOOK's Reliability

"How much of the Bible is true? How much is applicable today?" When asked these questions, I answer as follows: Unless you are comfortable calling God a liar or believe that He would inspire a lie, you must accept that it is all true. Here are some scriptural truths on this matter:

- *"All Scripture is given by inspiration of God, and is profitable for doctrine, for reproof, for correction, for instruction in righteousness, that the man of God may be complete, thoroughly equipped for every good work"* (2 Tim. 3:16–17).
- *"Paul, a bondservant of God and an apostle of Jesus Christ, according to the faith of the truth which accords with godliness, in hope of eternal life which God, who cannot lie, promised before time began . . ."* (Titus 1:1–2).
- *"Thus God, determining to show more abundantly to the heirs of promise the immutability of his counsel, confirmed it by an oath, that by two immutable things, in which it is impossible for God to lie, we might have strong consolation, who have fled for refuge to lay hold of the hope set before us"* (Heb. 6:17–18).
- *"God is not man, that He should lie. Nor a son of man, that He should repent, has He said, and will He not do? Or has He spoken, and will he not make it good? Behold, I have received a command to bless; He has blessed, and I cannot reverse it"* (Num. 23:19–20).

Is it even feasible for God to have ensured that flawed men would not pervert His Word by including myths in the Scriptures, or words that were not God-inspired?

Find assurance in these verses:

- *"And the Lord said to Abraham, 'Why did Sarah laugh, saying, "Shall I surely bear a child, since I am old?" Is there anything too hard for the Lord?'"* (Gen. 18:14).
- *"Behold, I am the Lord, the God of all flesh. Is there anything too hard for Me?"* (Jer. 32:26).
- *"But Jesus looked at them and said, 'With men it is impossible, but not with God, for with God all things are possible'"* (Mark 10:27).

How about the parts of THE BOOK that do not make sense or seem possible? How do you reconcile these things in your mind?

It is a mistake to try to understand God's Word through your mind, will, or emotions. God's message to us in Isaiah is clear: *"'For My thoughts are not your thoughts, nor are your ways My ways,' says the Lord. 'For as the heavens are higher than the earth, so are My ways higher than your ways, and My thoughts than your thoughts'"* (Isa. 55:8–9).

Thus, living in the Spirit is the key to this apparent dilemma: *"But the natural man does not receive the things of the Spirit of God, for they are foolishness to him; nor can he know them, because they are spiritually discerned"* (1 Cor. 2:14).

This verse from 1 Corinthians explains why prideful people with hard hearts, never fully understand THE BOOK. Perhaps this is why Jesus reacted in the manner He did when His disciples were arrogantly arguing about which of them was the greatest: *"Then Jesus called a little child to Him, set him in the midst of them, and said, 'Assuredly I say to you, unless you are converted and become as little children, you will by no means enter the kingdom of heaven. Therefore whoever humbles himself as this little child is the greatest in the kingdom of heaven'"* (Matt. 18:2–4).

As a leader, a human being, and a Christian, you are not going to take the Bible's mandate for moral righteousness seriously until you subordinate your pride and intellect to God's wisdom and do two things:

1. Acknowledge the relevance, inerrancy, and power of God's promises, warnings, rewards, and consequences for right and wrong behaviors.
2. Abrogate and decline to participate in modern society's rush toward the rationalization of sin and the debauchery in an age that responds to what God condemns with, "It's no big deal."

My goal in this chapter is to shine a spotlight on the pervasiveness and danger of these two key moral leadership failures. I do not have the qualifications, power, or ability to change you in these areas. That is God's work. My goal is to make you more aware of these dangers so that you are more compelled to avoid and overcome them. I also endeavor to help you understand the consequences to you and your organization should you decide — and these two threats *are* choices — to partake in them.

SEXUAL IMMORALITY TOPPLES THE STRONGEST, DEAREST, RICHEST, AND WISEST

There is no benefit to listing here the high-profile leaders and celebrities in recent memory who have committed acts of sexual immorality and thereby stained their legacy; destroyed their family; lost their fortune, office, and ministry; sunk their organization; humiliated their spouses, children, and followers; and dishonored God. While the failures of fallen celebrities grab headlines, sexual immorality diminishes people in every neighborhood, business, and religious institution and from each societal ethnic, economic, gender, and religious class.

By biblical definition, sexual immorality covers a lot of ground: adultery, fornication, homosexuality, lust, and more. Sexual immorality is also singled out for its significance because it involves sin against the body, which is the dwelling place of the Holy Spirit: *"Flee sexual immorality. Every sin that a man commits is outside the body, but he who commits sexual immorality sins against his own body. Or do you not know that your body is the temple of the Holy spirit who is in you, whom you have from God, and you are not your own? For you were bought at a price; therefore glorify God in your body and in your spirit, which are God's"* (1 Cor. 6:18–20).

The "It's no big deal" defense is the most common and ubiquitous rationalization for sexual failures. It is particularly downplayed, and in some cases promoted, on television and in the movies, which has made this sin appear normal—even cool to some degree. Lest you fall into the "It's no big deal" trap, consider how one aspect of sexual immorality—lust—affected THE BOOK's *strongest*, dearest, richest, and wisest men. Since it can be argued that lust is the catalyst for all sexual immorality, it is worth examining here.

Lust can be defined as "intense or unrestrained sexual craving. An overwhelming desire or craving: *a lust for power.* To have an intense or obsessive desire, especially one that is sexual."

In the workplace one may be tempted to lust for anything—power, position, money, and other material benefits, the corner office, or, of course, lust for flesh. We cover the sexual aspect here, citing scriptural references for you to explore on your own:

1. The world's strongest man, Samson, was defeated by lust (see Judges 16:1–4).
2. The man "after God's own heart," David—Israel's greatest king—was defeated by lust (see 2 Samuel 11:1–5).
3. The richest and wisest man who ever lived, King Solomon, was defeated by lust (see 2 Kings 11:1–4).

The fact that lust brought down some of the Bible's greatest heroes, men who were close to God, should get your full attention as you prepare to guard yourself against it in your own life.

One of my biblical mentors, Bill Gothard, relates the story of an ancient wrestling match that was particularly gruesome. Adrenaline flowed, because each man knew that if he lost the contest, his opponent would put a foot on his neck and call for a sword. The victor would then poke that sharpened sword into the eyes of his conquered foe.

Thereafter, the weaker wrestler would grope in blindness throughout the city as a public display of his defeat. This is a sobering introduction to the tremendous importance of one of Christ's most powerful and misunderstood commands concerning lust. *"Whosoever looketh on a woman to lust after her hath committed adultery with her already in his heart. And if thy right eye offend thee, pluck it out . . ."* (Matt. 5:28–29).

Peter speaks of this war when he writes: *"Dearly beloved, I beseech you as strangers and pilgrims, abstain from fleshly lusts, which war against the soul"* (1 Peter 2:11).

James explains the seriousness of this war as he asks, *"From whence come wars and fightings among you? Come they not hence, even of your lusts that war in your members?"* (James 4:1).

Paul describes the war within our members in very understandable terms: *"I see another law in my members, warring against the law of my mind, and bringing me into captivity to the law of sin which is in my members"* (Rom. 7:23). After explaining the war, Paul exclaims: *"O wretched man that I am! Who shall deliver me from the body of this death?"* (Rom. 7:24).

Peter also relates lust to eyesight when he gives a list of qualities that, if developed, will conquer lust, but, if missing, will cause us to be spiritually blind (see 2 Peter 1:1–19).

The tragedy of Samson's lust after women is also a sobering testimony. He lost the war on lust, his freedom, his leadership, and then he had his eyes gouged out (see Judges 16:20–21).

Besides the spiritual, marital, emotional, and physical penalties that come with lust, here are three other thoughts, warnings, and strategies for dealing with this potential time bomb in your workplace:

1. If you are a supervisor, you open yourself to claims of favoritism and sexual harassment when your lustful desires cause you to cross a line with one of your employees.
2. Lust is obsessive and possessive. The distractions that come with lustful fantasies reduce your effectiveness on the job, cloud your thinking, impair your judgment, and cause you to mismanage time as you become fixated on the object of your lust; meanwhile, you strategize ways to get closer to the object of your attention.
3. When you harbor affections that compete with those reserved for your spouse, whom you are commanded by God to love and respect, your relationship will suffer stress, coldness, emptiness, indifference, and strife. Try as you may, you cannot mask, disguise, or subdue your true feelings for long. What is in your heart will manifest itself in your speech, actions, and emotions.

The wrestler in our story may have been on his back, but as long as he had at least one shoulder above the mat, the fight was not over. If we are prone to surrender to lustful thoughts, now is the time to declare war against the giant of lust. He is one of our greatest adversaries against daily success. Memorizing passages in Romans 6–8 have proven for many to be particularly effective in controlling lustful impulses. Lust has a proven track record of destroying some of the most powerful and talented people in history. In light of this, do not be proud, ignorant, naive, or just plain foolish enough to think it cannot destroy you. As Peter warned us all, *"Be sober, be vigilant; because your adversary the devil walks about like a roaring lion, seeking whom he may devour"* (1 Pet. 5:8–9) (Gothard 2005).

Avoid and Remove Yourself from Potentially Vulnerable Situations

Many people wink at sin. They put themselves into unacceptable situations out of curiosity just to see what happens. This is an especially common practice for businesspeople as they travel.

As a very happily married man in my third decade of marriage, here are some rules I use that are designed to keep me out of vulnerable situations when my wife is not present:

1. I do not go into a hotel restaurant, lounge, or bar alone. Room service is convenient; pizza delivery is ubiquitous; and the protein drink mixes I travel with make a nutritious and filling meal.
2. I do not meet with a woman alone behind a closed door for any reason: business, small talk, or anything in between.
3. I do not surf Web chat sites just to make some new friends, nor do I peruse questionable web sites out of "innocent" curiosity.
4. Unless there is a pressing news story or a must-see sporting event, I rarely even turn on the television in a hotel room. I stay busy with reading and endless writing projects.
5. My personal computer has security software that tracks every site visited. The software company e-mails a weekly report detailing all Web activity on the computer. Family members are welcome to audit my reports and peruse my activity at any time. This sets an example for accountability throughout my household.

The moral: Even when you are not looking for trouble, trouble can find you, so do not put yourself in trouble's way! Those who flirt with disaster by uttering the worn-out clichés, "It never hurts to look," or "Ain't nothing wrong with looking," are playing with fire. Consider the cost of David's "look" as described in 2 Samuel 11.

King David merely walked out on the roof of his home one evening in apparent boredom to observe the kingdom and saw Bathsheba bathing. Here is a slide show of what happened next:

- He immediately desired her, summoned her to him, and got her pregnant.
- He had her husband killed.
- David's actions brought a curse upon his house.
- The baby that David and Bathsheba conceived together died a few days after birth.
- David was exposed by Nathan, the prophet, and repented before God and the entire kingdom.
- David's son, Absalom, had intercourse in public with 10 of David's concubines, which could be considered a tenfold retribution for David having taken another man's wife.
- Absalom fomented a rebellion against David that plunged the nation into civil war and resulted in Absalom's death.

JESUS IS YOUR TICKET OUT OF DARKNESS

If you have fallen into sexual immorality, right your course and sin no more.

In John 8, Jesus told the adulteress, *"Neither do I condemn you; go and sin no more"* (John 8:11). He then spoke to those He had been teaching in the temple and said, *"I am the light of the world. He who follows Me shall not walk in darkness, but have the light of life"* (John 8:12).

187

The true followers of Christ, those who have genuinely surrendered their lives to Him, will not continue in sexual immorality. They will not even want to. Once they genuinely commit to *follow* Jesus, they will walk out of the darkness of that sin and have the light of life He promises.

In 1 Corinthians 6, Paul offers a laundry list of sins, many of which involve sexual immorality. He then mentions that some of his readers used to do all of the things listed, but did them no longer because they were washed, sanctified, and saved by Christ. Take a look at this encouraging passage: *"Do you not know that the unrighteous will not inherit the kingdom of God? Do not be deceived. Neither fornicators, nor idolaters, nor adulterers, nor homosexuals, nor sodomites, nor thieves, nor covetous, nor drunkards, nor revilers, nor extortioners, will inherit the kingdom of God. And such were some of you. But you were washed, but you were sanctified, but you were justified in the name of the Lord Jesus and by the Spirit of our God"* (1 Cor. 6:9–11).

While this chapter has focused on the sexual failings of men, women should not make the error of believing the warnings, principles, and consequences herein don't apply to them. They do.

FALSE TEACHERS AND THEIR UNGODLY COUNSEL

The second threat to your leadership we cover in this chapter is the danger of false teachers and their ungodly counsel. Warnings of false teachers and their doctrine abound throughout the Bible.

- Jesus warned of false prophets who come in sheep's clothing, but inwardly are ravenous wolves. He told us that we would know them by their fruits (Matthew 7:15–16).
- Paul referred to them as "savage wolves," and warned the leaders in Ephesus that after he left them, they would come

in among them and draw away disciples to themselves (Acts 20:29–30).

- Peter cautioned that false teachers were coming and would bring with them dangerous heresies, that many would follow their dangerous ways, and that their greed would cause them to exploit followers with deceptive words (2 Peter 2:1–3).
- Jude warned that they had arrived and asserted that they had crept into the church unnoticed, turned the grace of God into lewdness, and denied the only Lord God and our Lord Jesus Christ (Jude 4).

Many professing Christians today chase after modern-day false teachers and their ungodly counsel. Oftentimes these deceiving spirits come in the form of "best practices," New Age philosophies, television gurus, authors, or high-profile "Christian" leaders. As a leader, you must follow the advice of 1 Thessalonians 5:23 and test these things through the filter of Christ and His Word. *"Test all things; hold fast what is good. Abstain from every form of evil."*

In other words, as a Christian, before you can even consider the worthiness of so-called teachers and what they espouse, you must apply two tests:

1. Does what they espouse align completely with biblical truth?
2. Does the teacher or teaching confess that Jesus Christ is God and that one attains salvation through Him and Him alone?

If the answer to either of these questions is no, you are confronting a false teacher. If the teachings of such people contradict, countermand, or compromise any aspect of God's Word, their message is not of God, it is of the devil. There is no in between, and there can be no compromise for an authentic Christian. Just as darkness is separate from light, this issue is just as starkly either black or white. If this paragraph makes you uncomfortable, it is because it contains something worthwhile to teach you. Open your mind and listen.

Modern False Teachers and Their Ungodly Doctrines

As I offer two of the many examples of false teachers and their teachings that have captivated the masses, including professing Christians, please keep in mind that this is but the tip of the iceberg. Use the two qualifying questions I listed previously to flush out more on your own. Then run in the opposite direction and return to biblical truth.

A Course in Miracles

In October of 1965, Helen Schucman, an atheist psychologist, began receiving channeled messages from an unknown spirit guide who claimed to be the voice of Jesus. Over time, Schucman wrote down what this voice told her, and it became the book embraced by high-profile personalities throughout the world, *A Course in Miracles* (Lutzer 2009).

This wildly popular course has 365 daily lessons that contradict the Bible and strip Christ of His Lordship. Its daily lessons have been sponsored by a popular talk show host and taught on XM satellite radio. This same sponsor has also actively promoted the teachings on her television show. Millions have fallen for the course's heretical success "principles." Here are a few samples that participants are encouraged to *say about themselves* and meditate on throughout the day:

Lesson #61: "I am the light of the world."

Lesson #96: "Salvation comes from my one Self."

Lesson #186: "Salvation of the world depends on me."

Lesson #191: I am the holy Son of God Himself" (Lutzer 2009, 22).

The *Course in Miracles,* also shares blasphemies like this: "The name of Jesus Christ as such is but a symbol. It is a symbol that is safely used as a replacement for the many names of all the gods to which you pray" (Lutzer 2009, 44).

And this . . . "The journey to the cross should be the last useless journey. Do not dwell upon it, but dismiss it as accomplished. . . . Do not make the pathetic error of clinging to the old rugged cross" (Lutzer 2009, 45).

There is no question in my mind that Helen Schucman did hear a voice that dictated this book to her. But it was certainly a voice from hell and not from Christ.

THE SECRET

The mega-best-seller *The Secret,* written by Rhonda Byrne and heavily promoted by television personalities, teaches that the key to getting whatever you want in your personal life or business is to use the "law of attraction," and to "think" these desires into existence. While Christianity teaches that Christ came in the flesh, Byrne claims that we are God in the flesh. She suggests that words that should be addressed to God are addressed to the person you see in the mirror each day. Needless to say, her message connected famously with today's generation, which is drowning in self-worship (Lutzer 2009, 32–33).

Many Christians have fallen for the New Age nonsense of *The Secret* as a way to go around Jesus and attempt to bring into their lives the things that He will not give to them fast enough! *The Secret* is nothing more than a doctrine of demons, as Paul described in his letter to Timothy, and which I included in the preface of this book. It is in the same category of New Age nonsense as *The New Earth, A Return to Love,* and *The Seat of the Soul.*

I can recall being at a business seminar at the height of *The Secret*'s popularity and listening in dismay as Christian businessmen boasted about how they used the law of attraction to get everything from an ideal parking space to a larger line of credit at their bank. They traveled with *The Secret,* but not with a Bible. They spent more time talking to the "universe" than they did speaking with Jesus. Like sheep led to slaughter, they are on their way to encountering what Jesus described in Matthew 7:21–23: *"Not everyone who says to Me, 'Lord, Lord,' shall enter the kingdom of heaven, but he who does the will of My Father in heaven. Many will say to Me in that day, 'Lord, Lord, have we not prophesied in Your name, cast out demons in Your name, and done many wonders in Your name?' And then I will declare to them, 'I never knew you; depart from Me, you who practice lawlessness.'"*

If you would like to educate yourself further on the pervasiveness of high-profile false teachers and their teachings, I highly recommend Dr. Erwin Lutzer's book, *Oprah, Miracles, and the New Earth: A Critique.*

LOOK IN THE MIRROR

The two threats I have listed here can be fatal to your leadership journey, within both your organization and your family. These threats are based on inside decisions, not on outside conditions. They start with your own power to choose, not with an event outside your control. They build a barrier between you and God, keeping you from His provision and spiritual protection.

At first glance, these two threats may seem very different from one another: sexual immorality versus false teachers and their ungodly teachings. However, they are identical in the sense that they can both become idols in your life. An idol is not necessarily a physical image that you worship. Rather, an idol is anything that absorbs more of your attention and affection than God. Lust, forbidden sexual fantasies and encounters, and New Age philosophies and doctrines can and do take center stage in a Christian's life and edge out God. Do not underestimate these threats. They are real. They are pervasive. They persistently crouch at your doorstep looking for an opening. It has been said that your biggest vulnerability is the one you are unaware of. After reading this chapter, the issue is no longer one of whether you know these things. The issue is, will you resist these things and remove yourself from unacceptable situations wherein these threats are likely to manifest? Paul and James both offer strong counsel in this regard:

- *"But put on the Lord Jesus Christ, and make no provision for the flesh, to fulfill its lusts"* (Rom. 14:13).
- *"Therefore submit to God. Resist the devil and he will flee from you"* (James 4:7).

Omega

"With her enticing speech she caused him to yield, with her flattering lips she seduced him. Immediately he went after her, as an ox goes to the slaughter or as a fool to the correction of the stocks, till an arrow struck his liver. As a bird hastens to the snare, he did not know it would cost his life" (Prov. 7:23–24).

1. Name the first two people who come to your mind when you think of sexual immorality? What can you learn from their error?
2. What false doctrines in the form of books, magazines, hobbies, self-help courses, or television gurus have you allowed to influence your life? What change will you now make to flee those forces and renounce them from your life?

"No temptation has overtaken you except such as is common to man; but God is faithful, who will not allow you to be tempted beyond what you are able, but with the temptation will also make the way of escape, that you may be able to bear it" (1 Cor. 10:13).

Closing Thoughts

Billions of dollars are spent each year to research why people behave in the dark manner they do and why the world is in so much trouble. It is not an oversimplification to answer that we have lost our will to submit to God and His ways. A Christian who does not submit to God is not much different than an atheist. While it can be argued that many atheists refuse to acknowledge the existence of God so they have an excuse to submit only to themselves and become their own god, what is a Christian's explanation for disobedience? If you believe in God but do not obey Him, are you more useful to Him than one who does not believe at all? Evangelist Charles Spurgeon wisely observed: "Worldly people may be of some use even if they fail in certain respects, but a counterfeit Christian is no longer good for anything, utterly useless to anybody and everybody" (Carter 1998, 106).

As this book concludes, here are two fair questions to consider. In your daily walk at work, in your community, church, and home, do you live your life in a way that makes you a "fisher of men," or is your life as a Christian failing to turn heads? Do you understand exactly what it means to be a fisher of men? It is exciting indeed!

In Jesus's day, fishing was much different than now. Fishermen like Peter, Andrew, John, and James would fish at night by shining lights into the water to attract fish. Once the fish were drawn to the light, they would drop their nets on them and sweep them into their boats. Thus, Jesus's command in Matthew 4:19, *"Follow Me and I'll make you fishers of men,"* takes on new meaning. Jesus wants us to act as a light in the world to draw others to Him through our actions, attitude, character, and love.

When you first meet Jesus, you begin to reflect His light. But after you place Him at the center of your life, build an intimate relationship, and follow His commands, you emit direct light that draws others to you and to Christ. This is exactly what Jesus meant when He declared, *"You are the salt of the earth"* in Matthew 5:13. Salt creates a thirst. When you lead and live by THE BOOK at work and in all areas of your life, you provoke a thirst in others that can only be quenched as they come to Christ's living water (Gothard 2005).

Thus, it is important to aspire to this lifestyle, as described by F. B. Meyer: "We ought to be Christians in large type, so that it would not be necessary for others to be long in our society, or to regard us through spectacles, in order to detect our true discipleship. The message of our lives should resemble the big advertisements which can be read on the street by all who pass by" (Richards 1990).

Aspire to be a "Christian in large type"! Remember what Jesus told us in Matthew 5:14: *"You are the light of the world. A city that is set on a hill cannot be hidden. Nor do they light a lamp and put it under a basket, but on a lamp stand and it gives light to all who are in the house. Let your light so shine before men that they may see your good works and glorify your Father in heaven."*

Thank you for taking this journey through *How to Lead by THE BOOK* with me. I have no doubt that there were sections that challenged you, even perhaps that you disagreed with. The fact that you persisted despite potential differences demonstrates a Christ-like attitude that celebrates unity and a willingness to focus on what we have in common, rather than on what makes us different.

May God guide you as you continue your Christian journey to live and love like Jesus in all sectors of your life; to be light; to be salt; to subordinate your own wisdom, desires, and agenda; and to submit to our all-powerful and flawless Lord.

Here is a special gift for you: At the conclusion of *How to Run Your Business by THE BOOK*, I offered readers a free one-year subscription to our electronic monthly newsletter of the same name. It expands upon the principles of both books, and it comes with a downloadable audio file suitable for your MP3 player. If you would like a free one-year subscription to this newsletter, please send an e-mail, with BTB NL in the subject line, to dave@learntolead.com. I would also be interested to read any comments about how this book has helped you.

One last thing . . . as you can imagine, even Christians may be hesitant to buy a book like this. They may feel it is too academic, preachy, touchy-feely, and the like. If you enjoyed and benefited from *How to Lead by THE BOOK*, please share a reader review on one of the many sites offering this option: Amazon.com, B&N.com, Goodreads, and more. Just a couple of lines from you could be the encouragement some people need to take the next step to help themselves or a loved one.

References

Preface

Lewis, C. S. *Mere Christianity*. San Francisco: HarperCollins, 2001.
Calvin, John. *Calvin's Commentaries*, vol. 19. Grand Rapids: Baker Books, 2005.

Chapter 3

Gothard, Bill. *Daily Success Course: Day 317*. Chicago: Institute in Basic Life Principles, 2005.

Chapter 4

Calvin, John. *Calvin's Commentaries*, vol. 21. Grand Rapids: Baker Books, 2005.

Chapter 6

Lewis, C. S. *Mere Christianity*. San Francisco: HarperCollins, 2001.
Simeon, Charles. *Expository Outlines on the Whole Bible*. Grand Rapids: Zondervan Publishing, 1955.

Chapter 10

Gothard, Bill. *Daily Success Course: Day 330*. Chicago: Institute in Basic Life Principles, 2005.

———. *Daily Success Course: Day 3—Be Cleansed by the Word*. Chicago: Institute in Basic Life Principles, 2005.

Chapter 14

Gothard, Bill. *Daily Success Course*. Chicago: Institute in Basic Life Principles, 2005.

Lutzer, Erwin. *Oprah, Miracles and the New Earth: A Critique*. Chicago: Moody Publishers, 2009.

Closing Thoughts

Carter, Tom. *Spurgeon's Commentary on Great Chapters of the Bible*. Grand Rapids: Kregel Publications, 1998.

Gothard, Bill. *Daily Success Course: Day 12—Fish with Light*. Chicago: Institute in Basic Life Principles, 2005.

Richards, Larry. *LivingChristian.net: The 365 Day Devotional Commentary*. November 30, 1990.

About the Author

Dave Anderson is the President of LearnToLead and an international speaker and trainer on leadership. He is the author of 12 books, including the Wiley titles *How to Run Your Business by THE BOOK, Revised and Expanded Edition*; *Up Your Business*; *If You Don't Make Waves You'll Drown*; *How to Deal with Difficult Customers*; and the TKO Business Series.

Dave, along with his wife Rhonda, are cofounders of the Matthew 25:35 Foundation, whose mission is to clothe, feed, house, educate, and bring healing and Christ to underresourced and imprisoned people throughout the world.

Visit www.learntolead.com for hundreds of free training articles, information on Dave's workshops, and other personal and corporate development material.

To book Dave to speak to your business or church group, contact Rhonda@learntolead.com or call 818-735-9503.

Dave and his family reside in southern California.

Index